THE KNIGHT BOOK OF THE WORLD CUP '74

Philip Evans has written two and a half novels, one of them with a football background; has contributed articles on football to the *Observer*, the *Sunday Times*, *World Soccer* and *Inside Football*; 'supports' the Italian club, Fiorentina; becomes manic whenever Barnsley win a game, and depressive whenever they lose; wishes that people in Britain were more knowledgeable about football as played overseas; and hopes that this brief book will prove something of a corrective.

THE KNIGHT BOOK OF THE

WORLD CUP '74

PHILIP EVANS

KNIGHT

he paperback division of Brockhampton Press

For Christopher and Penny

ISBN 0 340 18056 0

This edition first published 1973 by Knight, the paperback division of
Brockhampton Press, Leicester.
Text copyright © 1973 by Philip Evans

Printed and bound in Great Britain
by Cox & Wyman Ltd., London, Reading and Fakenham

CONTENTS

ACKNOWLEDGEMENTS

The author owes a great debt to Brian
Glanville for having written so much that is
trenchant about a fascinating sport; to
John Moynihan for much wit, wisdom and
wine; to Juliet Brightmore for having helped
put the thing together; and to Linda, if only
for Sampdoria – Napoli.

PROLOGUE

Approximately one thousand million people watched on television the Final of the 1970 World Cup tournament between Brazil and Italy; perhaps one third of the world's population. It's a staggering statistic, that; ample testimony to the grip that soccer has upon the lives and imaginations of so many people.

Of course, the availability of television has helped to spread the gospel. But the phenomenon was always there, if in embryonic form; and is there today, even in those countries where television is not part and parcel of the way of social life. Look at the growth and the spread of the game and you will see a recurring pattern – of enthusiasts taking up the game on an amateur basis, of crowds flocking to watch the sport, of the increase in the professionalism that inevitably followed, of interest on the part of the media.

Here are two quotes from very different writers, and making very different points; but both pointing to existing evils within the game. The first is from a novel entitled *The Harder They Fall* by the American Budd Schulberg and centred on the world of professional boxing – 'An athletic sport in an atmosphere of money is like a girl from a good family in a house of ill fame'. The second is from George Orwell, who markedly disapproved of international sport. Of it, he wrote, 'It is bound up with hatred, jealousy, boastfulness, disregard for all rules, and sadistic pleasure in witnessing violence – in other words, it is war minus the shooting'.

Now it is certainly true that the wealth inside football has often tended to introduce into it an element of greed. How many times have we all watched games in which the two sides seemed more intent on not losing than on actually

winning. That varies from match to match, country to country,
player to player. It is also true that matches between
international teams, between teams drawn from different
countries, have often degenerated into brawling, spiteful
battles. It is further true that players, officials and spectators
have been seriously injured, even killed, during the course
of games.

The fact is that the beauty of football lies in its simplicity;
that, whatever the experts decide, it will always be played by
twenty-two players kicking a piece of leather about a pitch.
It is that simplicity that gives it its drama, that helps to
highlight the particular characteristics of the players involved,
that invites fanatical participation on the part of crowds. One
of the fascinating facets of the 1966 World Cup finals, in
England, was the way in which we could all see the interest
shown in the game by people who had never seen a live
match. It didn't matter whether it was Miss Smyth who lived
in Hampstead, or Grandma Brown who lived in Bolton – both,
and many millions with them, were genuinely thrilled by
the *theatre* of what they watched on their television screens
each night: the guts and determination of Nobby Stiles, the
lithe elegance of Eusebio, the weaving runs of Albert – all
players of differing weight and talent, playing out their parts
on the world's largest stage.

I don't want to sound over-naïve and ingenuous about all
this, but the fact is that whenever the game is played really
well, people of all persuasions are readily prepared to make
their thanksgivings. Budd Schulberg and George Orwell may
well be right – but there is no need for anyone to accept
their statements lying down, as something that has to be
inevitable. It is probable that football will become richer
before becoming poorer and finding its rightful level in
financial terms as an entertainment for large crowds. But

international games do not have to be battles in disguise.
As with everything, you have to see the other person's point
of view. And if the approaching World Cup finals in Germany –
which will be the best yet organized – produce a winner as
universally popular as the 1970 Brazilians, if they throw up
a handful of games that are memorable, they will have served
their purpose in reminding millions of people throughout
the world that things are very much the same outside the
narrow confines of their own back gardens.

That is the real purpose of this book – to outline the good
and the bad left in the memory of history; and to invite a
little understanding.

1 A LOOK AT PREVIOUS TOURNAMENTS (1930-1954)

The idea of this book is to provide a readable and
(hopefully) interesting guide to what we all may hope to see
from what is known as the World Cup tournament to be
held in Germany during the summer of 1974. But before
getting to grips with the present it may be worth while to
recap on the events of previous tournaments.

One reason lies in the fascination of the past and the need
to realize that the great players of previous generations
might have been great whatever their date of birth. The other
is the more prosaic one of looking at power-balances. For
instance most people readily admit that over the last decade
and a half the Brazilians have been the players to most excite
spectators and coaches. But before the war Italy won the
World Cup twice; and throughout the history of the
tournament there have always been certain countries from
whom one could expect a high level of performance. The
Uruguayans have twice won the tournament, the Germans
have often featured strongly, and England's team of recent
years could never be taken lightly.

We might point out at the outset that 'the World Cup' is
something of a misnomer, that its proper name during the
years for which it was being competed was 'the Jules Rimet
Trophy'. The principle of an international tournament was
agreed in 1920 by FIFA – the Federation of International
Footballing Associations – and although it was ten years before
the first tournament came to be played, the guiding light
behind the idea and the man who most worked to get the
thing going was Jules Rimet, President of the French Football
Federation. Thus the attractive gold trophy came to be given
his name.

A sense of history might also help us to remember why the
achievement of British football in international terms has often
seemed so mediocre. The fact is that by 1930 – the year of
the first tournament – the four British associations (England,
Scotland, Wales and Northern Ireland) had all withdrawn
from FIFA and were thus ineligible to compete. In 1938 it
seemed that the rule might be waived and indeed England
were invited to compete in the Finals without having to
qualify, were offered the rôle of guest team in the absence of
Austria, overrun by the Nazis. The offer was refused, and it
was not until the first post-war tournament came to be played
in Brazil in 1950 that any of the British teams took part.

Even on that occasion, the seeming pig-headedness of the
administrators had its way. The British Home International
Championship preceding the Finals was recognized by FIFA
as a qualifying group, in which the first two could go through
to compete in the final stages. The Scots, amazingly, decided
that if they did not win the title, they would not go to Brazil.
The argument is one of those second-raters that seems
impressive in theory, very weak when one considers the rôle
of fortune in deciding so many sporting events – 'If we aren't
good enough to be more than second-best at home, why bother
to travel all that way and at that cost to prove that we are
second-best away'. The Scots lost 1-0 to England at Hampden,
and like Achilles sulking in his tent, stayed at home to lick
their wounds.

In fact the record of the Home Countries is not overly
impressive. True, England have recently been a most powerful
force, twice in the last eight and once winners over the past
three tournaments. But the English have been the only ones to
compete in all final stages since 1950. Scotland reached
through in 1954; and again four years later when the Welsh
and Irish also won through for their only taste of action after

the qualifying tournaments – and the only occasion in which
all four countries have been represented.

That twenty-year divorce between the teams drawn from the
four home countries and the major soccer tournament of the
world can be seen in retrospect to have been disastrous. It
became too easy to assume that because Britain had given
soccer in its modern form to the world, then naturally it had
to be more advanced, more skilful, more powerful than that
played overseas. True, in that period British teams often beat –
and handsomely – teams drawn from countries that had had
World Cup experience, and had proved that they could travel
away to do it. But it was always too easy to stay on the banks,
to pretend that British teams were the best without having
empirical proof. And come the first tournament for which
England qualified and they received their comeuppance in no
uncertain terms. With players such as Williams, Ramsey,
Wright, Dickinson, Finney, Matthews, Mortensen, Milburn
and Baily the English went to Brazil in 1950 as one of the
favourites and returned home humiliated. There were sad
reasons away from tactics and technique to explain the failure,
but the message was there for all to read, one that was
hammered home three years later by the Hungarians both at
home and away.

The fact is that, as with everything, you learn by watching,
by observing the skills and mistakes of others and British
teams were for twenty years denied this opportunity except in
'friendlies', games in which the natural aggression and will to
win of British players was too often not matched by a similar
guttiness on the part of their adversaries. If the British were
the ones to give soccer to the world, then the world soon
began to catch up and overhaul them. The pupil began to
show that he could outwit the master, and forced the latter
to get back to work himself. We should not be surprised then

to find in the history of the early World Cup tournaments no
mention of the British teams.

World Cup 1930 – held in Uruguay

Not unnaturally the first tournament was a strange affair.
Travel to Uruguay from Europe at the time was costly and
time-consuming. Little wonder then that so many of the
European competitors withdrew – Italy, Spain, Austria,
Hungary, Germany, Switzerland and Czechoslovakia among
them. In many ways one of the stars of the show proved to be
King Carol of Rumania – he not only picked the Rumanian
team, but ensured that the players were given adequate time
off from their firms. With only France, Belgium and
Yugoslavia of the other European countries being involved,
the affair was set for a South American victory.

When Uruguay as the place to hold a tournament such as
this? It seems strange; but the fact is that the Uruguayans had
taken the Olympic titles both in 1924 and 1928, they had
promised to build a handsome new stadium in which the
games could be played and had further guaranteed the
expenses of all the competing teams. Whether they were
bluffing on a withdrawal of most European teams or not, the
tournament went ahead, along the lines that have been common
recently – with teams playing initially in groups. Thirteen
countries competed in four pools, the winners of each pool
moving to the semi-final stage, together with the final played
on a knock-out basis.

When it came to it, two of the semi-finalists could be
ranked as surprises, one as a complete surprise. That was the
United States, for so long the chopping-block for skilful
South American teams in Olympic competition, but now able

to use some formidable ex-British professionals. In their first
game the Americans tanned Belgium 3-0; then beat Paraguay
by the same score and qualified for the semi-finals where they
would meet Argentina.

The Argentinians themselves had won their group without
dropping a point, but not before making enemies. They had
been outplayed for long stretches of their opening game against
the gallant French, took a one-goal lead and hung on to it
thanks to some bizarre refereeing. With six minutes of the
game remaining, Langiller, the French left-winger, ran almost
the length of the pitch only for the Brazilian referee to whistle
full-time just as he reached the opponents' penalty area. The
French complained, the game was eventually restarted, but
the damage had been done. For the Argentinians there then
came a game against Mexico, won by six goals to three, with
the referee awarding five penalties. And then a 3-1 defeat of
Chile to take them through to the next stage.

The other semi-finalists were Yugoslavia – winners by 2-1
over Brazil and 4-0 over Bolivia; and the host team, Uruguay
who scratched and scraped to find their form before going
through against Peru 1-0 and then took the Rumanians to the
cleaners by four goals to none. The stage was set for the South
Americans to face the invaders.

In the event, the semi-finals were an anti-climax. Against a
skilful and ruthless Argentinian team, the strength and brawn
of the United States team proved ineffective – they went
down by six goals to one. And in the other game, the
Uruguayans thrashed Yugoslavia by the same score.

Both victorious teams were undoubtedly strong. The
Uruguayans had prepared for the tournament with a dedication
that has recently been commonplace, then considered
extraordinary, one that made nonsense of any thought that
they were still amateurs. For two celibate months the players

had been trained ruthlessly, deprived of freedom, a rigorous
curfew imposed on their nocturnal wanderings. When their
brilliant goalkeeper, Mazzali, was discovered late one night,
shoes in hand, sneaking in after a night on the town he was
thrown out and his place given to a reserve.

There has never been much love lost between South
American teams on the football field, and the natural rivalry
that already existed between Uruguay and Argentina had
recently been pointed by the defeat of the latter at the hands
of the former in the final of the 1928 Olympic tournament.
If the Uruguayans had a formidable half-back line in Andrade,
Fernandez and Gestido, if they had a great fullback in their
captain, Nasazzi, if they had superb technicians in their
forward-line such as Scarone and Petrone, then their
adversaries were similarly equipped with some fine individual
performers. Monti, the Argentinian centre-back was a ruthless
and skilful destroyer – a player who could block out opposing
strikers with awesome tactics. At centre-forward they had the
ingenious Stabile, who was to be the tournament's leading
scorer with eight goals – a man who earned and lived up to
the nickname of El Infiltrador – the man who could wriggle
his way through the most packed of defences. And for their
later games they had the services of the genuine captain and
another skilful striker in Manuel Ferreira.

The Final, strangely, was played in a comparatively peaceful
way, the Uruguayans winning by four goals to two after having
trailed by the odd goal in three at half-time. Off the field and
after the game came the expected Argentinian protests – that
the Uruguayans had been 'brutal', that the referee had been
bought. Relations between the footballing authorities of the
two countries were broken off. But the first World Cup had
been played – and won handsomely by a very good team.

1930 – Final Stages

Semi-Finals

ARGENTINA 6, UNITED STATES 1 (1-0)

ARGENTINA: Botasso; Della Torre, Paternoster; Evaristo, J.,
Monti, Orlandini; Peucelle, Scopelli, Stabile, Ferreira (capt.),
Evaristo, M.
USA: Douglas; Wood, Moorhouse; Gallacher, Tracey, Auld;
Brown, Gonsalvez, Patenaude, Florie (capt.), McGhee.
SCORERS: Monti, Scopelli, Stabile (2), Peucelle (2) for
Argentina; Brown for USA.

URUGUAY 6, YUGOSLAVIA 1 (3-1)

URUGUAY: Ballesteros; Nasazzi (capt.), Mascheroni; Andrade,
Fernandez, Gestido; Dorado, Scarone, Anselmo, Cea, Iriarte.
YUGOSLAVIA: Yavocic; Ivkovic (capt.), Mihailovic; Arsenievic,
Stefanovic, Djokic; Tirnanic, Marianovic, Beck, Vujadinovic,
Seculic.
SCORERS: Cea (3), Anselmo (2), Iriarte for Uruguay; Seculic for
Yugoslavia.

Final

URUGUAY 4, ARGENTINA 2 (1-2)

URUGUAY: Ballesteros; Nasazzi (capt.), Mascheroni; Andrade,
Fernandez, Gestido; Dorado, Scarone, Castro, Cea, Iriarte.
ARGENTINA: Botasso; Della Torre, Paternoster; Evaristo, J.,
Monti, Suarez; Peucelle, Varallo, Stabile, Ferreira (capt.),
Evaristo, M.

SCORERS: Dorado, Cea, Iriarte, Castro for Uruguay; Peucelle,
Stabile for Argentina.

World Cup 1934 – held in Italy

Four years later, the competition was altogether more
representative and better attended. The Uruguayans stayed
away – piqued by the refusal of so many European teams to
grace their tournament in 1930; and the Argentinians, having
lost too many of their star players to Italian clubs, came with
something of a reserve side. More important was the
background to the tournament, played in Fascist Italy.

Mussolini and his henchmen were in no doubt – if the Italian
team could provide good results, even win the tournament,
what a blow that would be in propaganda terms. It took a lot
of haggling before Italy was chosen as the host country, but
once given the job of organizing the competition, the Italians
went to work like demons, losing no opportunity to get
across the Fascist theme in propaganda literature, in posters,
in the Press. Mussolini's features stared up from the official
booklets, stared down from the Tribune of Honour in the
various stadia.

In the event, the Italians had a fine team, pulled together by
Vittorio Pozzo, a remarkable manager. It contained three
Argentinians of supposed Italian extraction – the fearsome
Monti, whom we've met before, among them. They were
included on the justification that if they were eligible to do
military service for Italy, they were eligible to play football
for Italy. From the start Pozzo proved himself a master
psychologist – and he needed to be. He was dealing with
temperamental stars of great technical ability in individual
terms, little will to play with and for each other. Pozzo it was

who welded together a squad of seeming disparates by locking
the players up in ritiro, forcing them to live and train closely
together, matching the prima donna antics of the one against
those of the other, until all came to feel that they were being
treated equally. In Combi, the Italians had a superlative
goalkeeper; they had Monti; and in the forward line they had
the 'new' discovery, Giuseppe Meazza. Although the strong
Austrian *wunderteam* was there, although Hungary and Spain
could be fancied, many things pointed towards a second
victory in the tournament for the team playing at 'home'.

In fact, there were several organizational changes from the
first tournament. Whereas all the games in Uruguay had been
played in the new stadium, purpose-built in Montevideo, it
had been realized that in future more than one city would be
needed to accommodate all the games. In Uruguay, thirteen
teams had competed; here there were sixteen, this complete
turnout allowing a change in the formula so that the
tournament was a knock-out affair from first to last; and the
cities that were graced by first-round ties were eight – Rome,
Naples, Florence, Milan, Turin, Bologna, Genoa and Trieste.

The gallant Americans were there, ready to prove that their
performance in 1930 had been no flash in the pan; but they
met Italy in the first round and lost by seven goals to one.
Spain, with the fabulous Zamora in goal, beat Brazil 3-1; the
Germans, another team not to be under-valued, beat Belgium
5-2; Austria scraped through against France by the odd goal in
five and after extra time; and Hungary revenged the bitter
humiliation of having lost to Egypt in the 1924 Olympiad. On
to the second round, with Italy and Spain drawn against each
other.

Zamora was much feared, a goalkeeper who in the past had
too often barred the way of Italian forwards not to be taken
seriously, even at his current age of thirty-three. In the event

he played a superb game, plucking centres and corner-kicks
out of the air with sure timing and adhesive hands. But his
courage had a price to be paid. Although he withstood 120
minutes of pressure as the game – stymied at 1-1 – moved
into extra time, there seemed little chance at the final whistle
that he would be fit to play on the succeeding day when
the replay was due to take place.

Nor did he. And although the Spanish held Italy to just the
one goal, they had been forced to field five other reserves.
When played, the second game was even more pathetically
refereed, so badly that the Swiss official concerned was
suspended by his own federation. The Italians were through,
but with that smear of luck that successful teams will always
need to make their point.

To join them in the semi-finals came Germany – well
organized in defence, and fortunate that the Swedes were down
to ten men for much of their 2-1 victory; Austria, who beat
Hungary by the same score in a brawling game that could
never have suited the Austrians' penchant for swift, close
passing; and Czechoslovakia, who came through against
Switzerland 3-2.

That left Italy to face the fancied Austrians only two days
after that bruising replay against Spain, and though there was
only the one goal in their favour, their command was
seldom in question. The Austrians were forced to wait until
the forty-second minute before even aiming a shot at goal.

In the Final, the Italians came face to face with Czechoslovakia,
much too clever for the Germans in the previous round, and
were given a real run for their money. The Czechs took the
lead through Puc in the middle of the second half, soon after
missed two golden chances and hit a post. You shouldn't be
allowed such freedom in competition, and much to their
dismay the Czechs found Italy equalizing with only eight

minutes to go – a freak goal from Orsi, struck with his right
foot and curling wickedly in the air. (The following day in
practice, he tried twenty times – without success – to repeat
it.) In the seventh minute of extra time, the Italians scored the
winning goal through Schiavio and that was that – victory
snatched from the enterprising Czechs just when they seemed
to have the thing in the bag.

   Neutral experts were eager to make their points. The
advantage of home ground, they pointed out, had been
decisive (it always is, surely); the frenzied, para-military
support; the consequent intimidation of referees – these all
may have been decisive. They may, but no one doubted that
the 'World Cup' was now firmly established, on the road to
improvement in terms of organization and skill.

1934 – Final Stages

Semi-Finals

CZECHOSLOVAKIA 3, GERMANY 1 (1-0). *Rome*

CZECHOSLOVAKIA: Planika (capt.); Burger, Ctyroky; Kostalek,
Cambal, Krcil; Junek, Svoboda, Sobotka, Nejedly, Puc.
GERMANY: Kress; Haringer, Busch; Zielinski, Szepan (capt.),
Bender; Lehner, Siffling, Conen, Noack, Kobierski.
SCORERS: Nejedly (2), Krcil for Czechoslovakia; Noack for
Germany.

ITALY 1, AUSTRIA 0 (1-0). *Milan*

ITALY: Combi (capt.); Monzeglio, Allemandi; Ferraris IV,
Monti, Bertolini; Guaita, Meazza, Schiavio, Ferrari, Orsi.

AUSTRIA: Platzer; Cisar, Sesztar; Wagner, Smistik (capt.),
Urbanek; Zischek, Bican, Sindelar, Schall, Viertel.
SCORER: Guaita for Italy.

Third Place Match

GERMANY 3, AUSTRIA 2 (3-1). *Naples*

GERMANY: Jakob; Janes, Busch; Zielinski, Muensenberg,
Bender; Lehner, Siffling, Conen, Szepan (capt.), Heidemann.
AUSTRIA: Platzer; Cisar, Sesztar; Wagner, Smistik (capt.),
Urbanek; Zischek, Braun, Bican, Horwath, Viertel.
SCORERS: Lehner (2), Conen for Germany; Horwath, Seszta for
Austria.

Final

ITALY 2, CZECHOSLOVAKIA 1 (0-0) (1-1) after extra time. *Rome*

ITALY: Combi (capt.); Monzeglio, Allemandi; Ferraris IV,
Monti, Bertolini; Guiata, Meazza, Schiavio, Ferrari, Orsi.
CZECHOSLOVAKIA: Planika (capt.); Zenisek, Ctyroky; Kostalek,
Cambal, Krcil; Junek, Svoboda, Sobotka, Nejedly, Puc.
SCORERS: Orsi, Schiavio for Italy; Puc for Czechoslovakia.

World Cup 1938 – held in France

Again the tournament was played in several venues, again it
was played along strictly knock-out lines, again it was won by
Italy. And won more convincingly, it must be said. As if to
prove that their football was the best in the world, the Italians

had entered for, and won, the 1936 Olympiad – aided by the
use of dubious 'amateurs', aided by the unpleasant Nazi
ambience; but still a further victory to point to, further
evidence that they had emerged as a powerful side.

Pozzo was still at the helm; to join Meazza in the forward
line was Silvio Piola – a tall, powerful centre-forward who
would score so many goals in Italian league football and for
the international team; in place of the uncompromising
Monti, Pozzo had at his disposal another South American
hatchet-man in Andreolo of Uruguay; and to replace Combi in
goal was yet another excellent keeper in Olivieri.

If victory in 1934 had been important to the Italians as a
propaganda weapon, success in 1938 was deemed no less
important and for the same reason. Political interest reared
its head elsewhere. The Argentinians refused to come because
they had not been given the competition; Spain was forced to
withdraw on account of the bloody Civil War; and the
Austrians – their country having been swallowed up by the
Nazis – found themselves without a team for which to play.
In fact, the 'German' team comprised seven players from
Germany, four from Austria. Ironic, therefore, that in the first
round this combined outfit should have to face the Swiss – as
neutral a country as was possible in the succeeding war.

The first game went to 1-1; the replay panned out to a
Swiss victory by four goals to two. Trailing by the odd goal
in three into the second half, all seemed lost to the Swiss when
they lost a player through injury. Not a bit of it. They waited
for his return, equalized soon after, and then ran through for
two more goals.

There were other surprises in store, given the context of
history. The Dutch East Indies took part – annihilated by a
formidable Hungarian side 6-0; and Cuba played well enough
– beating the Rumanians after a replay in the first round – for

us to wonder what has happened to Cuban football in the last
three decades. Italy made heavy weather of Norway, winning
by the odd goal in three after extra time; and in an
extraordinary game, again needing extra time to decide the
outcome, the Brazilians beat Poland 6-5. Playing at centre-
forward for the South Americans that day – and scorer, like
the Pole, Willimowski, of four goals – was Leonidas, the
Black Diamond, a player of extraordinary reflex and lightning
anticipation. On to the second round.

The Cubans came a great cropper at the hands of
Sweden, losing 8-0; the Hungarians, with the mercurial Sarosi
at centre-forward, put out gallant Switzerland 2-0; the Italians,
their morale revived by the cunning Pozzo, and thanks to two
goals from Piola, beat France 3-1; and the fireworks were
reserved for the game between the Brazilians and the Czechs.

It was nothing less than a holocaust, with three players –
two of them Brazilians – sent off, and two more retiring to
hospital with broken limbs. Not for nothing was the game to
be known as the 'Battle of Bordeaux', not for the last time was
the tension of a great occasion to prove too much for the
Brazilians. They ran out of spirit in the second half, after
Leonidas had given them the lead, gave away a penalty and the
world rubbed its hands or shielded its eyes in expectation of
the replay.

In the event, the affair was peaceful, mild to an amazing
degree. The Brazilians made nine changes, the Czechs six;
Leonidas scored yet again, equalizing the opening goal from
the Czechs, and Roberto it was who tucked away the winner.

And then came even more crazy an episode. Drawn against
the Italians, the Brazilian team manager announced that
Leonidas and Tim – his two great goal-scorers – would miss
the semi-final round and were being 'kept for the final'.
Nobody believed him, of course; but when the teams ran on to

the pitch – no Leonidas, no Tim. Hamlet without the Prince
and Horatio indeed; and playing straight into the hands of
the Italians. They scored the first two of the three goals in the
game, were seldom under hard pressure.

In the other semi-final Sweden scored a goal within the first
thirty-five seconds of play, then crumpled before the vaunted
Hungarian attack, who scored five times, thrice before half-
time. So dominant was the play of the central Europeans that
for much of the second half a large blackbird sat peacefully
on the field of play twenty yards away from the Hungarian
goalkeeper.

Italy against Hungary in the Final, then; but first the play-off
for third place, and the salt really rubbed into Brazilian
wounds. Leonidas returned and scored two goals in a 4-2
victory over Sweden, posing questions that might have
overtaxed the Italian defence had he ever been given the
chance to ask them of it, and running out as the tournament's
top scorer.

The Final itself seemed to be symbolized by the struggle
between two great centre-forwards; Piola for Italy, Sarosi for
Hungary. For all the skill of the latter, it was the bite and
drive of the former that proved decisive. Two early goals
within a minute provided a dramatic beginning; then the
bustling style of the Italians took them into a two-goal lead.
Hungary came back with twenty minutes to go through Sarosi,
threatened briefly, then went under finally with ten minutes
to play when Piola drove in the Italian's fourth goal.

Italy had unquestionably deserved her triumph this time.
And the World Cup would remain in Italian hands for twelve
long years while the world went to war and many players of
talent died violent deaths.

1938 – Final Stages

Semi-Finals

ITALY 2, BRAZIL 1 (2-0). *Marseilles*

ITALY: Olivieri; Foni, Rava; Serantoni, Andreolo, Locatelli;
Biavati, Meazza (capt.), Piola, Ferrari, Colaussi.
BRAZIL: Walter; Domingas Da Guia, Machados; Zeze, Martin
(capt.), Alfonsinho; Lopex, Luisinho, Peracio, Romeo, Patesko.
SCORERS: Colaussi, Meazza (penalty) for Italy; Romeo for Brazil.

HUNGARY 5, SWEDEN 1 (3-1). *Paris, Colombes*

HUNGARY: Szabo; Koranyi, Biro; Szalay, Turai, Lazar; Sas,
Szengeller, Sarosi (capt.), Toldi, Titkos.
SWEDEN: Abrahamson; Eriksson, Kjellgren; Almgren, Jacobsson,
Svanstroem; Wetterstroem, Keller (capt.), Andersson H.,
Jonasson, Nyberg.
SCORERS: Szengeller (3), Titkos, Sarosi for Hungary; Nyberg
for Sweden.

Third Place Match

BRAZIL 4, SWEDEN 2 (1-2). *Bordeaux*

BRAZIL: Batatoes; Domingas Da Guia, Machados; Zeze,
Brandao, Alfonsinho; Roberto, Romeo, Leonidas (capt.),
Peracio, Patesko.
SWEDEN: Abrahamson; Eriksson, Nilssen; Almgren, Linderholm,
Svanstroem (capt.); Berssen, Andersson H., Jonasson,
Andersson, A., Nyberg.

SCORERS: Jonasson, Nyberg for Sweden; Romeo, Leonidas (2),
Peracio for Brazil.

Final

ITALY 4, HUNGARY 2 (3-1). *Paris, Colombes*

ITALY: Olivieri; Foni, Rava; Serantoni, Andreolo, Locatelli;
Biavati, Meazza (capt.), Piola, Ferrari, Colaussi.
HUNGARY: Szabo; Polgar, Biro; Szalay, Szucs, Lazar; Sas, Vincze,
Sarosi (capt.), Szengeller, Titkos.
SCORERS: Colaussi (2), Piola (2) for Italy; Titkos, Sarosi for
Hungary.

World Cup 1950 – held in Brazil

Twenty years had elapsed since the tournament was last held
in South America, and the problems thrown up had not, it
appeared, been diluted. Thirteen teams had completed in
1930, the tally in 1950 would be no larger. The Indians
qualified, but would not come; Scotland, as we have seen,
fatuously stayed out; the Austrians were going through one of
their frequent bouts of diffidence, and felt their team not
strong enough (even though they had just beaten Italy – who
would play); Hungary, like the Russians, remained in Cold
War isolation; the French, knocked out in their qualifying
group, and then reprieved, felt the journey too long and
arduous; and the Argentinians had squabbled with the
Brazilian Federation. As for West Germany, they were still
barred from FIFA.

Thirteen teams, then; and the gaps made nonsense of the
new pool system, which would apply not merely to the four
qualifying groups, but also to the final group – competed in
by the four winners. The Uruguayans, for example, had only
to play one jog-trot of a game to be through to the final
pool – a victory by eight goals to none over Bolivia. Little
wonder that they seemed more fresh and zestful in the late
stages of the tournament.

The massive Maracana stadium in Rio de Janeiro was still
being built when the tournament started – and when it
finished. Brazil featured there in the opening match, beating
Mexico by four clear goals in front of a happily partisan crowd
of 155,000 (the Maracana would hold 200,000). Two of
their goals came from Ademir – yet another of those
incredible ball-playing inside forwards that the Brazilians had
a penchant for producing. Like the Uruguayans in 1930, the
Italians in 1934, the Brazilians had prepared with military
thoroughness – an air of celibacy and special diets reigned
supreme. They would qualify for the final pool – but not
before drawing against Switzerland with a mis-chosen team,
and having to fight very hard against a determined Yugoslavian
side.

Co-favourites with Brazil were – England! Appearing for the
first time in the competition, with some devastating form
behind them, the English had to be fancied. Whatever the
balance of power suggested, eyes turned interestedly towards
them. They had yet to find a centre-forward to replace
Lawton, but Matthews was there, Finney was there, Mortensen
was there, Mannion was there; and these were players whose
skill was legendary. They scraped through their first game
against Chile, finding the heat and humidity so oppressive
that they took oxygen at half-time. And then came the shock
of the tournament – possibly one of the greatest shocks in the

history of international football – as England went down by
just the one goal to the United States.

A number of the American players had stayed up into the early
hours of the morning; several of them expected a cricket
score, and indicated as much to British journalists. In the
event, it was eight minutes before half-time when Gaetjens
headed in Bahr's cross (or was it a miskicked shot?); and that,
whatever the English forwards would do in the second half,
remained the only goal of the match. The victory of Chile
over the Americans a few days later and by five goals to two
emphasized England's shame. And although Matthews and
Milburn were brought in for the final English game against
Spain, although many felt the English deserved at least a draw,
the die was cast. England were out of a tournament whose
previous editions they had ignored, one for which they had
been heavily favoured.

Into the final pool along with Spain, Brazil and Uruguay
went Sweden. They had won the 1948 Olympic tournament
with a team that included Gren, Nordhal and Liedholm – all,
alas, now playing in Italy and blocked from selection. What
irony, then, that in their first game the Swedes should play the
Italians and win by the odd goal in five! A draw against the
other team in their pool, Paraguay, and Sweden were through.

Little good it was to do them, with Brazil now turning on
all the fireworks. In their first game the Brazilians beat
Sweden 7-1; in their second, Spain by 6-1. Their trio of inside
forwards – Jair, Ademir and Zizinho – seemed uncontrollable:
professional counterparts of those countless boys who juggle
footballs on the Copacabana beach from sunrise to sunset.
Brazil, it seemed, would handsomely win the title.

The challenge came from Uruguay, held to a draw by Spain,
victors over Sweden (who would in turn defeat the Spanish
with that perverse logic that accompanies these affairs). If the

Brazilians had Jair, Ademir and Zizinho – the Uruguayans had
Juan Schiaffino, as thin as a piece of paper, a player of
enormous technical skills that would later be appreciated by
European audiences when he found his way into the cauldron
of Italian league football, once described by Tommy
Docherty (the present manager of Manchester United) as the
best player he ever had to face.

But for all Schiaffino's skills, the Uruguayans were the first
to admit that they were unable to match the Brazilians in
terms of pure technique. Tactical expertise was needed, and
tactical expertise was used. Hard as they might try, the
Brazilian forwards seldom seemed able to penetrate the
light-blue defensive barrier thrown up by the Uruguayan
defence, the dark mastery of Maspoli in the opposing goal.
No score at half-time.

Two minutes after the interval, the Maracana erupted as
Friaca closed in from the wing, shot – and scored. But the
Uruguayans had made their point, knew that they were able to
cope with the 'superteam' that opposed them. Schiaffino it
was who put them ahead, ghosting through the centre to knock
in a cross. And ten minutes before the end, Ghiggia, the
Uruguayan left-wing, cut in, beat his fullback to score.

The 'right team' had lost; Uruguay had won a match of
breath-taking quality and the tournament for a second time
after an interval of twenty years.

1950 – Final Stages

Final Pool

URUGUAY 2, SPAIN 2 (1-2). *São Paulo*

URUGUAY: Maspoli; Gonzales, M., Tejera; Gonzales, W., Varela
(capt.), Andrade; Ghiggia, Perez, Miguez, Schiaffino, Vidal.
SPAIN: Ramallets; Alonzo, Gonzalvo II; Gonzalvo III, Parra,
Puchades; Basora, Igoa, Zarra, Molowny, Gainza.
SCORERS: Ghiggia, Varela for Uruguay; Basora (2) for Spain.|

BRAZIL 7, SWEDEN 1 (3-1). *Rio*

BRAZIL: Barbosa; Augusto (capt.), Juvenal; Bauer, Danilo,
Bigode; Maneca, Zizinho, Ademir, Jair, Chico.
SWEDEN: Svensson; Samuelsson, Nilsson, E.; Andersson,
Nordahl, K., Gard; Sundqvist, Palmer, Jeppson, Skoglund,
Nilsson, S.
SCORERS: Ademir (4), Chico (2), Maneca for Brazil; Andersson
(penalty) for Sweden.

URUGUAY 3, SWEDEN 2 (1-2). *São Paulo*

URUGUAY: Paz; Gonzales, M., Tejera; Gambetta, Varela (capt.),
Andrade; Ghiggia, Perez, Miguez, Schiaffino, Vidal.
SWEDEN: Svensson; Samuelsson, Nilsson, E.; Andersson,
Johansson, Gard; Johnsson, Palmer, Melberg, Skoglund,
Sundqvist.
SCORERS: Palmer, Sundqvist for Sweden; Ghiggia, Miguez (2) for
Uruguay.

Keystone Press Agency

A tight situation from the 1954 'Battle of Berne' between Brazil and Hungary. From left, Nilton Santos (Brazil), Castilho (Brazil), Toth (Hungary) and Brandaozinho (Brazil). Santos was later sent off for fighting, together with Boszik, the Hungarian captain.

From the 1954 Hungary–Uruguay semi-final. Hidegkuti scores the second Hungarian goal as Maspoli, the Uruguayan goalkeeper, looks on in alarm.

United Press International

Left: From the 1954 final. Morlock, the German centre-forward scores the first of his side's goals in their unexpected 3-2 victory over the Hungarian 'wunderteam'.

Above: World Cup Final, 1954. Puskas (Hungary) has put the ball in the net with moments to go before full-time. But the 'goal' is disallowed, and Germany win the tournament.

Above: World Cup 1954. Ferenc Puskas of Hungary congratulates the German captain, Fritz Walter after the final. Looking on is Jules Rimet, former FIFA President.

Right: World Cup 1958. The gallant Welsh drew 0-0 in their qualifying group with Sweden, eventual finalists. Here the legendary John Charles forces Svensson to a save, with full-back Axbom in attendance.

Keystone Press Agency

United Press International

Left: From the 1958 final. The amazing Garrincha centres for Vavà (No. 20) to hammer in Brazil's first, and equalizing, goal.

Above: World Cup 1958. The victorious Brazilian team. From left to right. *Standing:* Trainer, Djalma Santos, Zito, Bellini, Nilton Santos, Orlando, Gilmar. *Kneeling:* Garrincha, Didi, Pelé, Vavà, Zagalo, trainer. All but Bellini and Orlando would play four years later; and these two would be mysteriously recalled in 1966.

World Cup 1954 – held in Switzerland

And here was another instance of the 'wrong' team coming
through to take the trophy, when Germany won their first
World Cup and the brilliant Hungarians (possibly the best
team Europe has yet seen) were denied their right. Bizarre
organization in which two teams from each group were
'seeded', leaving the supposedly stronger teams apart in the
early stages; and the presence of a handful of really formidable
teams in Hungary, Brazil, Germany, Uruguay and Austria –
both these ensured that in later years this would come to be
known as the last of the 'open' tournaments, the last in which
teams seemed more concerned to score, than to prevent, goals.

England were there, shaky after a hammering administered
at the hands of the Hungarians only a couple of weeks earlier
when their winter defeat at Wembley had been exposed as no
fluke. In Budapest they lost 7-1, a disorganized rabble in front
of brilliant passing and shooting. History was on their side,
Matthews, Wright and Finney in it; but few gave them any
chance. And Scotland were also there – having repeated one
part of their rôle from 1950 by losing to England; this time,
however, having the courage to enter in spite of their lack of
confidence.

Uruguay were strong, entering their first European tournament,
unbeaten to date. Schiaffino was still there; they had splendid
new wingers in Abbadie and Borges; a powerful stopper in
Santamaria, later to be the bulwark of Real Madrid's invincible
side. The Brazilians were slightly fancied despite being involved
in a period of neurotic assessment. Their game, they felt, was
too ingenious; so they closed the defence with care, came
down hard on flair unless it could be harnessed to teamwork.

They would wait until 1958 before perfecting the balance, but
in their first game of the tournament – a 5-0 drubbing of
Mexico – they introduced two great backs in the Santoses
(no relation), a fine distributor in Didì, a unique winger in
Julinho – a man of violent pace, superb balance, close control
and with a rocket of a shot.

In their first game, the Uruguayans beat the Czechs 2-0; then
annihilated Scotland by seven clear goals, Broges and Abbadie
getting five between them. The Scottish campaign had not been
helped by dissension off the pitch and the resignation, after
the first defeat at the hands of Austria, of Andy Beattie, the
team manager; but the Uruguayans looked good, Schiaffino in
regal form. Through to join them in the quarter-finals went
Yugoslavia – who had held Brazil to a 1-1 draw in a memorable
match in which their goalkeeper Beara (a former ballet dancer)
had performed prodigies in defence and Zebec had given
evidence of his all-round skill; England, drawing 4-4 with
Belgium first time out before beating Switzerland 2-0; the
Swiss, thanks to a played-off game against the Italians, who
had been strangely static; Brazil; Austria, who defeated the
Czechs 5-0 with their talented half-back Ocwirk emerging as
one of the players of the tournament; Germany and Hungary.

This last pair provided most of the news. The Hungarians
went out in their first game, drubbed Korea 9-0; then were
forced to play the Germans, the latter not having been seeded.
The wily German coach, Sepp Herberger, cleverly decided to
throw away this match, banked on winning the play-off against
Turkey (which he did) and fielded a team largely composed of
reserves. The Hungarians came through 8-3, the Germans had
not given away any secrets; but most important, it was in this
game that Puskas was injured, that a vital part of the Hungarian
machine was put out of action.

The Hungarians had won the 1952 Olympiad; in Hidegkuti

they had a deep-lying centre-forward of great verve and
authority, a man who could make and score brilliant goals; at
inside forward they had Kocsis and Puskas, the former a little
man with the neck of a bull who could leap great heights to
head a ball, the latter with a hammer of a left foot; and in
the half-back line they had an excellent exemplar in Boszik,
always driving forward with speed, ingenuity and strength.
With four players of genius and others who were little behind,
it was easy to see why the Hungarians were widely considered
favourites to win the tournament.

Two things upset them. First, the injury to Puskas, who would
play again only in the Final and at half-speed. The other was
what came to be known as the 'Battle of Berne', a disgraceful
quarter-final tie which pitted them against the Brazilians.
Hungary won the game 4-2 after being two up in the first
eight minutes, after giving away a penalty, after themselves
scoring from one, after Nilton Santos and Boszik had been
sent off for fighting in a match that seemed more suited to a
boxing ring. After the game the Brazilians invaded the
Hungarian dressing-room, went berserk, and came close to
inflicting further serious injury on the Hungarian players.
Hungary were through to the semi-finals where they would
play an unforgettable game against Uruguay, victors over an
England team that fought hard, laid siege to the Uruguayan
goal without really capitalizing on their approach play (where
Matthews was outstanding) and was let down by Merrick, the
goalkeeper.

The other semi-final would be between Austria who beat
Switzerland 7-5 after having trailed 2-4 at half-time; and
Germany, ploughing on with force and thoroughness against
the talented Yugoslavs. In the event, the Germans 'came good'
when it mattered. They scored twice from penalties in their
6-1 win, now seemed ominously hard to beat.

The Hungary–Uruguay game, even without Puskas, was a
gem. Two-nil up with fifteen minutes to go, the Hungarians
seemed through – until the Uruguayans counter-attacked.
Schiaffino put Hohberg through, the move was repeated three
minutes before the end, and extra time was on. It nearly began
without Hohberg himself, who had been forced to retire
'injured' after having been overwhelmed by delighted team mates.
But recover he did, to burst through early in the first period of
extra time and smack in a shot – that came back off a post.
In retrospect, it can be seen as the turning point; for Kocsis
twice in the second period rose to head home crosses; and
Hungary were through.

A Puskas far from fit, too chubby round the middle and with
a sore ankle, returned for the Final. Great player though he
was, the Hungarians had managed well without him, and
might have done better to discard him (as Alf Ramsey would
prefer Roger Hunt to Jimmy Greaves twelve years later,
sacrificing rare gifts to teamwork, and win). Yet again, the
Hungarians went off like a train, two goals up in eight
minutes, seemingly well on the way to a victory that awaited
them.

What mattered most, perhaps, was the swiftness of the German
reply. Three minutes later they had drawn back a goal
through Morlock; then Rahn drove home a corner; at the other
end Turek remained in stupendous form between the goalposts;
Rahn got the goal that would be the winner; Puskas scored –
only to be given offside; and the invincible Hungarians had
been beaten.

They had been beaten by a better team on the day; by the
punishment of earlier games against South Americans; by a
certain amount of internal dissension to do with the injury to
Puskas. Yet they remained the best team that Europe had seen
to date, possibly the best team that Europe has yet seen. And

it took an almost equally brilliant team from the other side of
the world and four years later, to push them into the light
shadows; the amazing Brazilians of the Sweden tournament,
and their latest wonder-boy – Pelé.

1954 – Final Stages

Quarter-Finals

GERMANY 2, YUGOSLAVIA 0 (1-0). *Geneva*

GERMANY: Turek; Laband, Kohlmeyer; Eckel, Liebrich, Mai;
Rahn, Morlock, Walter, O., Walter, F. (capt.), Schaefer.
YUGOSLAVIA: Beara; Stankovic, Crnkovic; Cjaicowski I, Horvat,
Boskov; Milutinovic, Mitic (capt.), Vukas, Bobek, Zebec.
SCORERS: Horvat (own goal), Rahn for Germany.

HUNGARY 4, BRAZIL 2 (2-1). *Berne*

HUNGARY: Grosics; Buzansky, Lantos; Boszik (capt.), Lorant,
Zakarias; Toth, M., Kocsis, Hidegkuti, Czibor, Toth J.
BRAZIL: Castilho; Santos, D., Santos, N.; Brandaozinho, Pinheiro
(capt.), Bauer; Julinho, Didi, Indio, Tozzi, Maurinho.
SCORERS: Hidegkuti (2), Kocsis, Latnos (penalty) for Hungary;
Santos, D. (Penalty), Julinho for Brazil.

AUSTRIA 7, SWITZERLAND 5 (2-4). *Lausanne*

AUSTRIA: Schmied; Hanappi, Barschandt; Ocwirk (capt.),
Happel, Koller; Koerner, R., Wagner, Stojaspal, Probst,
Koerner, A.
SWITZERLAND: Parlier; Neury, Kernen; Eggimann, Bocquet
(capt.), Casali; Antenen, Vonlanthen, Hugi, Ballaman, Fatton.

SCORERS: Ballaman (2), Hugi (2), Hanappi (own goal) for
Switzerland; Koerner, A. (2), Ocwirk, Wagner (3), Probst for
Austria.

URUGUAY 4, ENGLAND 2 (2-1). *Basel*

URUGUAY: Maspoli; Santamaria, Martinez; Andrade, Varela
(capt.), Cruz; Abbadie, Ambrois, Miguez, Schiaffino, Borges.
ENGLAND: Merrick; Staniforth, Byrne; McGarry, Wright (capt.);
Dickinson; Matthews, Broadis, Lofthouse, Wilshaw, Finney.
SCORERS: Borges, Varela, Schiaffino, Ambrois for Uruguay;
Lofthouse, Finney for England.

Semi-Finals

GERMANY 6, AUSTRIA 1 (1-0). *Basel*

GERMANY: Turek; Posipal, Kohlmeyer; Eckel, Liebrich, Mai;
Rahn, Morlock, Walter, O., Walter, F. (capt.), Schaefer.
AUSTRIA: Zeman; Hanappi, Schleger; Ocwirk (capt.), Happel,
Koller; Koerner, R., Wagner, Stojaspal, Probst, Koerner, A.
SCORERS: Schaefer, Morlock, Walter, F. (2 penalties), Walter, O.
(2) for Germany; Probst for Austria.

HUNGARY 4, URUGUAY 2 (1-0) (2-2) after extra time.
Lausanne

HUNGARY: Grosics; Buzansky, Lantos; Bostik (capt.), Lorant,
Zakarias; Budai, Kocsis, Palotas, Hidegkuti, Czibor.
URUGUAY: Maspoli; Santamaria, Martinez; Andrade (capt.),
Carballo, Cruz; Souto, Ambrois, Schiaffino, Hohberg, Borges.
SCORERS: Czibor, Hidegkuti, Kocsis (2) for Hungary; Hohberg
(2) for Uruguay.

Third Place Match

AUSTRIA 3, URUGUAY 1 (1-1). Zürich
AUSTRIA: Schmied; Hanappi, Barschandt; Ocwirk (capt.),
Kollman, Koller; Koerner, R., Wagner, Dienst, Stojaspal, Probst.
URUGUAY: Maspoli; Santamaria, Martinez; Andrade (capt.),
Carballo, Cruz; Abbadie, Hohberg, Mendez, Schiaffino, Borges.
SCORERS: Stojaspal (penalty), Cruz (own goal), Ocwirk for
Austria; Hohberg for Uruguay.

Final

GERMANY 3, HUNGARY 2 (2-2). Berne
GERMANY: Turek; Posipal. Kohlmeyer; Eckel, Liebrich, Mai;
Rahn, Morlock, Walter, O., Walter, F. (capt.), Schaefer.
HUNGARY: Grosics; Buzansky, Lantos; Boszik, Lorant (capt.),
Zakarias; Czibor, Kocsis, Hidegkuti, Puskas, Toth, J.
SCORERS: Puskas, Czibor for Hungary; Morlock, Rahn (2) for
Germany.

2 BRAZIL, BRAZIL, ENGLAND, BRAZIL (1958-1970)

World Cup 1958 – held in Sweden

The Brazilians came and conquered – came to Sweden as one of the favourites (thanks to the on-paper banality of much of the opposition), conquered with an extraordinary demonstration of prowess and skill in the Final. The backstage people concerned, for the first time, harnessed the natural talent of the players, made the team's play really effective. In 1950 the players had been allowed to express themselves too freely; in 1954, they had been too restrained. Now the blend was right.

Yet the truth remains, that like the Hungarians before them but to a lesser degree, the Brazilians proved that great teams – so called – depend essentially upon the coming-together in one period of time of a clutch of great players. Didì was in evidence again, full of lithe passes, famous for his 'falling leaf' shot – struck with the outside of the foot and fading distressingly in midflight; the Santoses were playing still at fullback; and in the forward line were two new geniuses in Garrincha and the new black prodigy, Pelé. And there was Zagalo, a player who covered vast tracts of ground at electric pace, one with lungs of leather and an astute footballing brain. The components were there, and the world waited to see whether they could be put together.

All four British teams competed; the Welsh and Irish for the first and – to date – last time. The former had a fine goalkeeper in Kelsey, the majestic John Charles, a clever inside-forward in Allchurch, an impish winger in Cliff Jones. The latter had Danny Blanchflower and Jimmy McIlroy, but the Munich air disaster had deprived them of Blanchflower's brother, Jackie, a

commanding centre-back. Both teams thrived on the intimate
atmosphere they created for themselves off the field, devoid of
the paranoia and bitching that had surrounded English team
selection.

To be fair to England, they had suffered terribly from
Munich. The accident deprived them of Duncan Edwards, their
brilliant left-half; Tommy Taylor, a dangerous centre-forward;
and Roger Byrne, a resourceful back. Players such as these
could not be replaced overnight, admittedly; but some of the
selection was bizarre in the extreme. Lofthouse was left at
home, when his experience might have been invaluable; and
Bobby Charlton, whose amazing swerve and lethal shooting
had delighted everyone in the previous three months, was
taken – only to be left on the touchlines for the whole
tournament. Courage, it seemed, was lacking – the courage that
often wins matches and tournaments.

The Scots had eliminated Spain but lost 4-0 to England in
Glasgow. Few held out for them much hope of success. The
Hungarians had lost too many of their star players in the
aftermath of the 1956 Revolution, and such as remained were
long in the tooth. Argentina competed, but without its much-
famed 'Trio of Death' in the inside forward positions –
Maschio, Angelillo and Sivori – all playing with Italian clubs
and ignored. And the Germans seemed weak, despite the
continued and cunning presence of Herberger, the coach.

The Russians competed for the first time, having won the
1956 Olympiad in Australia. They had the amazing Yachin in
goal, kept themselves to themselves, and would play the sturdy
sort of game that one has come to expect from them in recent
years – functionalism with just the occasional flash of forward
and midfield genius.

Playing at home, the Swedes called upon several of their stars
based in Italy – the elegant Liedholm, tall and commanding in

midfield; Nacka Skoglund, a hero of their 1950 World Cup team; Gustavsson, a commanding centre-back; and Kurt Hamrin, an electric little outside-right. To begin with, their supporters were pessimistic, but pessimism soon changed to optimism.

No one anticipated much from the French, yet they were to be the revelation of the tournament. In their first game, they walked through Paraguay 7-3, three of the goals coming from Juste Fontaine, who had come to the tournament not expecting to gain a place. He would score thirteen goals in all – a record that will not easily be beaten. And alongside Fontaine was Kopa – small, strong, beautifully-balanced with fine control and the ability to give a defence-splitting pass.

Group IV was the focal point – Brazil, Russia, England and Austria. The Brazilians beat the other two, drew a goalless game against England, who also drew with Russia and Austria. To a play-off, and the Russians came through by the one goal. If only Tom Finney had not been injured in the first game of the tournament. If only.

The Irish drew against the Germans, beat the Czechs, lost to Argentina – who finished bottom of the pool! They came through after a play-off against Czechoslovakia, by the odd goal in three, with McParland scoring his second goal of the game in the first period of extra time. Courage, in their case, had paid off.

The Scots drew with Yugoslavia, went down to both France and Paraguay. Better news from the Welsh, who went to a play-off in their pool against the Hungarians – and won 2-1 after trailing at half-time. The victory would put them through against Brazil, and few gave them much hope.

That especially after the 'real' Brazil had played for the first time in the third game of their qualifying group. Out had gone Jose Altafini, nicknamed 'Mazzola' for his resemblance

to the great post-war Italian inside forward; a man who would
play for Italy in the 1962 finals, who at the age of thirty-four
would score against Derby County in the semi-final of the
1972-73 European Cup trophy goals that were *par excellence*,
those of a venomous striker. And in would come Garrincha
and Pelé.

Both were to have an extraordinary effect on the 1958
competition, an extraordinary effect on players and spectators
throughout the world. Garrincha and Pelé – two of the great
instinctive players of the age, of any age. The former was a
winger who had all the powers of Matthews – the vicious
swerve that took him outside the full back, the ability to
accelerate into astonishing speed from a standing start. Despite
– perhaps because of – a curiously twisted knee, a legacy from
birth, his ball-control was exceptional. And Pelé, at seventeen,
his head pointed like a coconut, with all his legendary skills
already there for all to see – the ability to 'kill' a ball on thigh
or chest, to shoot ferociously from impossible angles, to head a
ball with a power that reminded people of Lawton or Kocsis.

So what chance Wales, against players such as these? In the
event, much. If only John Charles had been fit to play, the
one Welshman who could have put pressure on the Brazilian
defence. As it was, the Welsh defence played superbly; and
Pelé was later to describe the one goal of the match as the
most important he had ever scored. And there's over a
thousand from which to choose!

Into the semi-finals with Brazil went France, Germany,
Sweden. The Germans churned on, their ageing team and
cunning management able to find answers to all the questions
posed by the Yugoslavs. Sweden went through with Hamrin
on venomous form – stockings rolled down, small and
compact, hard to stop once he began to find his stride, scorer
of the first goal against the Russians, maker of the second.

And there was France – the team no one was prepared to take
seriously, even though they had won their qualifying group and
scored eleven goals in the process. Against the Irish, Fontaine
scored twice more to re-emphasize his effectiveness. Tired and
depleted by injuries, the Irish had no cause for complaint. Their
effort, like that of the Welsh, had been brave and dignified.

In the semi-finals, it was the turn of the French to suffer at
the hands of Brazil. The score was still 1-1 when Jonquet, the
elegant French centre-half was forced to retire in the thirty-
seventh minute: a retirement that was to prove fatal as Pelé
scored a hat trick and Brazil ran out winners 5-2. France
would have consolation later, when they would defeat Germany
in the match to decide third place by six goals to three, four
coming from the incessant Fontaine.

Germany had proved no match for Sweden. The raucousness
of German chanting at international matches is legendary, but
in Sweden the German supporters found their match. As the
Swedes progressed from round to round, so grew the noise of
their fans, nationalist to the extreme. And so on the field, the
Germans could find no answers to the wiles of Liedholm in
midfield, the venom of Hamrin as he cut in from the wing.
They would unearth a potentially great defender in Schnellinger,
a powerful midfield player in Szymaniak – but the Germans
knew that they deserved to be out.

In the Final, the Swedish crowd was silenced by FIFA. An
official had attended the semi-final game, put a stop to organized
cheering . . . and a Swedish crowd deprived of its cheerleaders
would scarcely cheer at all. Just the once, as Liedholm put
Sweden ahead after four minutes. 'When the Brazilians are a
goal down,' had said George Raynor, Sweden's Yorkshire coach,
'they panic all over the show.' But Raynor must have been
thinking of the overtrained 1954 Brazilians or the dazzling
unpredictables of 1950.

Twice, it was Garrincha; twice he swerved maniacally past
Swedish defenders and centred; twice Vavà rushed in to score.
And ten minutes after half-time it was Pelé's turn. Trapping a
long centre on his thigh, he hooked it over his head, slashed
it into the net. He would score Brazil's fifth goal with his head
after Zagalo had torn through for the fourth. And though
Sweden would get a second goal, that would be that.

The crowd applauded as the Brazilians did two laps of
honour, first with their own flag, then with that of the Swedes.
Their supporters chanted 'samba, samba'. And the world knew
that it had seen a new style of football.

1958 – Final Stages

Quarter-Finals

FRANCE 4, IRELAND o (1-o). Norrkoping

FRANCE: Abbes; Kaelbel, Lerond; Penverne, Jonquet, Marcel;
Wisnieski, Fontaine, Kopa, Piantoni, Vincent.
IRELAND: Gregg; Keith, McMichael; Blanchflower, Cunningham,
Cush; Bingham, Casey, Scott, McIlroy, McParland.
SCORERS: Wisnieski, Fontaine (2), Piantoni for France.

GERMANY 1, YUGOSLAVIA o (1-o). Malmö

GERMANY: Herkenrath; Stollenwerk, Juskowiak; Eckel, Erhardt,
Szymaniak; Rahn, Walter, Seeler, Schmidt, Schaefer.
YUGOSLAVIA: Krivocuka; Sijakovic, Crnkovic; Krstic, Zebec,
Boskov; Petakovik, Veselinovic, Milutinovic, Ognjanovic,
Rajkov.
SCORER: Rahn for Germany.

SWEDEN 2, RUSSIA 0 (0-0). *Stockholm*

SWEDEN: Svensson; Bergmark, Axbom; Boerjesson, Gustavsson,
Parling; Hamrin, Gren, Simonsson, Liedholm, Skoglund.
RUSSIA: Yachin; Kessarev, Kuznetsov; Voinov, Krijevski, Tsarev;
Ivanov, A., Ivanov, V., Simonian, Salnikov, Ilyin.
SCORERS: Hamrin, Simonsson for Sweden.

BRAZIL 1 WALES 0 (0-0). *Gothenburg*

BRAZIL: Gilmar; De Sordi, Santos, N.; Zito, Bellini, Orlando;
Garrincha, Didì, Mazzola, Pelé, Zagalo.
WALES: Kelsey; Williams, Hopkins; Sullivan, Charles, M.,
Bowen; Medwin, Hewitt, Webster, Allchurch, Jones.
SCORER: Pelé for Brazil.

Semi-Finals

BRAZIL 5, FRANCE 2 (2-1). *Stockholm*

BRAZIL: Gilmar; De Sordi, Santos, N.; Zito, Bellini, Orlando;
Garrincha, Didì, Vavà, Pelé, Zagalo.
FRANCE: Abbes; Kaelbel, Lerond; Penverne, Jonquet, Marcel;
Wisnieski, Fontaine, Kopa, Piantoni, Vincent.
SCORERS: Vavà, Didì, Pelé (3) for Brazil; Fontaine, Piantoni for
France.

SWEDEN 3, GERMANY 1 (1-1). *Gothenburg*

SWEDEN: Svensson; Bergmark, Axbom; Boerjesson, Gustavsson,
Parling; Hamrin, Gren, Simonsson, Liedholm, Skoglund.
GERMANY: Herkenrath; Stollenwerk, Juskowiak; Eckel,
Erhardt, Szymaniak; Rahn, Walter, Seeler, Schaefer, Cieslarczyk.
SCORERS: Schaefer for Germany; Skoglund, Gren, Hamrin for
Sweden.

Third Place Match

FRANCE 6, GERMANY 3 (0-0). *Gothenberg*

FRANCE: Abbes; Kaelberl, Lerond; Penverne, Lafont, Marcel;
Wisnieski, Douis, Kopa, Fontaine, Vincent.
GERMANY: Kwiatowski; Stollenwerk, Erhardt; Schnellinger,
Wewers, Szymaniak; Rahn, Sturm, Kelbassa, Schaefer,
Cieslarczyk.
SCORERS: Fontaine (4), Kopa, penalty, Dous for France;
Cieslarczyk, Rahn, Schaefer for Germany.

Final

BRAZIL 5, SWEDEN 2 (2-1). *Stockholm*

BRAZIL: Gilmar; Santos, D., Santos, N.; Zito, Bellini, Orlando;
Garrincha, Didì, Vavà, Pelé, Zagalo.
SWEDEN: Svensson; Bergmark, Axbom; Boerjesson, Gustavsson,
Parling; Hamrin, Gren, Simonsson, Liedholm, Skoglund.
SCORERS: Liedholm, Simonsson for Sweden; Vavà (2), Pelé (2),
Zagalo for Brazil.

World Cup 1962 – held in Chile

It should, perhaps, have been held in the Argentine. But if
Chile had recently suffered serious earthquakes, then the
general antipathy towards Argentina in footballing circles had
not lessened. And as the Chileans put it, they needed the
World Cup *'because* we have nothing'. Cunning logic, indeed;
and the Chileans set about building a fine stadium in Santiago
to house a hysterical populace. (Cynics pointed out that

Chile had won nothing since the Pacific War in the middle of
the nineteenth century.)

Brazil were the favourites, inevitably. They had two new
centre-backs; and that was all. Garrincha, Zagalo, Didí and Pelé
were still there – though the last would play only two games
before being replaced by another exciting striker in Amarildo.
And taken seriously with the Brazilians were the Russians – who
on a recent South American tour had beaten Argentina,
Uruguay and Chile.

England had played well on their way to Chile, beating Peru
4-0 in Lima. In Greaves and Charlton they had world class
forwards; in Bobby Moore, a debutant in Lima, a defender of
poise. But the self-confidence was not there, the forwards would
fail time and again to find a way through the packed defences
that would make a nonsense of the early part of the competition.

Italy arrived with Gianni Rivera in their ranks, arguably one
of the really gifted players Europe has seen since the end of
the war. Eighteen then, a precision passer of the ball and with
a perfect sense of balance he would play one good game
before being dropped. The Italians also brought with them a
host of Oriundi – foreigners of Italian extraction – such as
Altafini, Sormani, Maschio and Sivori. A strong team on paper,
but football matches are not won on paper – and the Italian
campaign would be catastrophic.

After a goalless draw against Germany, the Italians found
themselves involved in yet another of those World Cup 'battles'
when they came to play Chile in Santiago. At the root of the
trouble were some silly newspaper articles written by Italian
journalists, critical of the organization of the tournament,
critical of the squalor of Santiago, critical of the morals of
Chilean womanhood. From the start of the game the Chileans
spat at the Italians, fouled them viciously. Ironic, therefore, that
the two players sent off in the game should both have been

Italian; while a left hook thrown by Sanchez, the Chilean
winger – one that broke Maschio's nose – went unseen by the
referee. Two-nil to Chile, and the Italians were effectively out
of the tournament.

Germany won that second group, with Schnellinger powerful
in defence, Seeler powerful in attack, Szymaniak destroying
everything in midfield. They had come up with a useful
inside-forward in Helmut Haller, who would find fame in
Italy in later years and compete in two further World Cups.
And the Chileans, inevitably, came through.

In group III, Brazil beat Mexico 2-0; were held to a goalless
draw by the unfancied Czechs – a game in which Pelé pulled a
muscle, and was lost to the rest of the tournament; then beat
Spain, with Amarildo – Pelé's replacement – getting both goals
in a 2-1 victory. The Czechs went through even though they
had lost one of their games, drawn another.

In group I, the Russians won a violent yet exciting game against
Yugoslavia 2-0; then were involved in an extraordinary match
against the Colombians, who after being 3-0 down in the first
fifteen minutes took the final score to 4-4. Yachin in goal had a
sad game, sad enough for some commentators to prophesy the
end of the greatest goalkeeper of modern times. Premature indeed,
if only for Yachin's fine displays in England four years later.
Yugoslavia would go through to the quarter-finals with Russia,
their little inside-forward, Sekularac, one of the men of the
tournament.

And so to group IV, where the Hungarians looked a fine side.
In Florian Albert they had unearthed a centre-forward of high
gifts, another who would do marvellously in 1966. And in
Solymosi, the right-half, they had a player of relaxed quality.
These two were highly responsible for the 2-1 defeat of the
English side in the first game; the 6-1 thrashing administered
to Bulgaria in the second.

As for England, they played good football – with Bobby
Charlton on great form – to defeat the Argentinians 3-1. Alan
Peacock made his debut, and a fine one. But in the final game
against the Bulgarians, the English could find no way through
a massed defence, had to be content with a goalless draw.
They were through, but few would dare to class them with the
Hungarians.

In the event, they met – and were beaten by – Brazil. The
3-1 scoreline seemed slightly unjust; but Garrincha was in
devastating form, seemingly having added to his vast repertoire
of tricks the ability to head a ball viciously. And though Hitchens
equalized for England before half-time, two mistakes by Springett
in goal gave goals to Vavà and Amarildo after the interval.

No surprise, that result, but surprises elsewhere. Chile, for
example, came through against Russia – with Yachin still
inexplicably tense in goal, and the crowd manic in its joy.
Not for the first or last time, the 'home' team had confounded
early prognostication.

And Hungary went out. For eighty of the ninety minutes
against the Czechs Hungary attacked, inflicting serious damage
on the Czech crossbar and posts. Nothing, it seemed, would
ever be a few millimetres farther in the right direction; and
though Solymosi and Albert did everything that was asked of
them, their team ever trailed to an early, thirteenth-minute
goal from the Czech inside-forward, Scherer.

In the last quarter-final tie, the Yugoslavs put out the
Germans. Only four minutes of the game remained when Galic,
the inside-left, dribbled his way through the German defence
and passed to Radakovic – head bandaged after a collision –
to score. But the Germans could have had little reason for
complaint. In Sekularac, the Yugoslavs had one of the best
midfield players of the tournament; in Soskic a strong, agile
goalkeeper; in Markovic, a commanding centre-back, who on

the day would outplay the formidable Uwe Seeler.

In the semi-finals, it was the turn of Chile to fall before the devastating Garrincha. He scored the first of four Brazilian goals with a fierce left-foot shot, the second with another of his new-found trampoline-like headers. And though the Chileans hit back with a goal before half-time from Toro, two further goals – this time from Vavà – in the second half, and only a penalty in return, put the Brazilians through.

Not, however, without tremblings. In the second half of the game Garrincha himself was expelled for kicking retaliatorily at a Chilean opponent; and then suffered the indignity of having his head cut open by a bottle thrown from the crowd as he was leaving the pitch. In the event, the injury was not serious, the threat of suspension from the Final very real. It was said, however, that the President of Brazil had listened to the game on headphones during Mass; that he had appealed personally to the disciplinary committee on Garrincha's behalf. The brilliant winger would play in the Final after receiving a caution.

The opposition to Brazil would be provided by the Czechs, victors in the other semi-final against Yugoslavia. As in the quarter-final, the Czechs had much less of the play; but this time took their chances well, scoring three goals, conceding one. Masopust controlled the midfield; the other two half-backs, Pluskal and Popluhar, sealed up the middle of the defence with rugged authority; Kvasniak ambled round in the forward line prompting and guiding. And the weary Yugoslavs were left to lose the match for third place, by the one goal and against a Chilean side again whipped on by a partisan crowd.

As in 1958, Brazil gave away the first goal of the Final – Masopust scoring in the fourteenth minute after having run on to an exquisite through pass from Scherer; as in 1958, the team's reaction was swift and interesting. It was Pelé's

replacement, Amarildo, who scored, running almost to the
left-hand goal line with the ball, screwing an extraordinary
shot past Schroiff, the Czech goalkeeper, who had positioned
himself perfectly at the near post to narrow the angle.

One-one, then, at half-time; and when Brazil scored again in
the sixty-ninth minute, good goal though it was, it came
against the run of the play. Amarildo it was who collected a
pass from Zito, cut past a defender and crossed for Zito
himself to charge in and head just under the bar. Thus was
the slightly one-paced elegance of Masopust and Kvasniak
rewarded; and salt was further rubbed into the wound twelve
minutes from time when Djalma Santos hooked a centre high
into the Czech penalty area, Schroiff lost its flight against the
glare of the sun, lost it when it hit the ground, and Vavà
snapped in to score, 3-1, seemingly a convincing win; but
Garrincha had been well controlled, Didì had been obscure.

Brazil had won the Cup for the second time, but with little of
the flair that they had shown in Sweden. True, Pelé had been absent
for the important games, and Pelé might have made a considerable
difference. The Brazilians, however, had been forced to use Zagalo
as a deep-lying winger, and the 4-2-4 formation of 1958 had
wilted into the 4-3-3 of 1962, would even tempt people to think
of four midfield players and only two genuine strikers.

More serious, it had been a disappointing tournament. The
great Puskas, taking time off from scoring goals for his new
club, Real Madrid, said of the football he had seen that it
was 'war'. The qualifying games had provided a string of
disappointments, defensive skill had been at a premium. The
tournament in Sweden had provided 119 goals, that in Chile
thirty less; and where Fontaine had scored so freely in 1958,
the highest figure that any individual goalscorer would reach
in Chile was four.

1962 – Final Stages

Quarter-Finals

YUGOSLAVIA 1, GERMANY 0 (0-0). *Santiago*

YUGOSLAVIA: Soskic; Durkovic, Jusufi; Radakovic, Markovic,
Popovic; Kovacevic, Sekularac, Jerkovic, Galic, Skoblar.
GERMANY: Fahrian; Novak, Schnellinger; Schultz, Erhardt,
Giesemann; Haller, Szymaniak, Seeler, Brulls, Schaefer.
SCORER: Radakovic for Yugoslavia.

BRAZIL 3, ENGLAND 1 (1-1). *Viña del Mar*

BRAZIL: Gilmar; Santos D., Mauro, Zozimo, Santos, N.; Zito,
Didì; Garrincha, Vavà, Amarildo, Zagalo.
ENGLAND: Springett; Armfield, Wilson; Moore, Norman,
Flowers; Douglas, Greaves, Hitchens, Haynes, Charlton.
SCORERS: Garrincha (2), Vavà for Brazil; Hitchens for England.

CHILE 2, RUSSIA 1 (2-1). *Arica*

CHILE: Escutti; Eyzaguirre, Contreras, Sanchez, R., Navarro;
Toro, Rojas; Ramirez, Landa, Tobar, Sanchez, L.
RUSSIA: Yachin; Tchokelli, Ostrovski; Voronin, Maslenkin,
Netto; Chislenko, Ivanov, Ponedelnik, Mamikin, Meshki.
SCORERS: Sanchez, L., Rojas for Chile; Chislenko for Russia.

CZECHOSLOVAKIA 1, HUNGARY 0 (1-0). *Rancagua*

CZECHOSLOVAKIA: Schroiff; Lala, Novak; Pluskal, Popluhar,
Masopust; Pospichal, Scherer, Kvasniak, Kadraba, Jelinek.
HUNGARY: Grosics; Matrai, Sarosi; Solymosi, Meszoly, Sipos;
Sandor, Rakosi, Albert, Tichy, Fenyvesi.
SCORER: Scherer for Czechoslovakia.

Semi-Finals

BRAZIL 4, CHILE 2 (2-1). *Santiago*

BRAZIL: Gilmar; Santos, D., Mauro, Zozimo, Santos, N.; Zito,
Didì; Garrincha, Vavà, Amarildo, Zagalo.
CHILE: Escutti; Eyzaguirre, Contreras, Sanchez, R., Rodriguez;
Toro, Rojas; Ramirez, Landa, Tobar, Sanchez, L.
SCORERS: Garrincha (2), Vavà (2), for Brazil; Toro, Sanchez, L.
(penalty) for Chile.

CZECHOSLOVAKIA 3, YUGOSLAVIA 1 (0-0). *Viña del Mar*

CZECHOSLOVAKIA: Schroiff; Lala, Novak; Pluskal, Popluhar,
Masopust; Pospichal, Scherer, Kvasniak, Kadraba, Jelinek.
YUGOSLAVIA: Soskic; Durkovic, Jusufi; Radakovic, Markovic,
Popovic; Sujakovic, Sekularac, Jerkovic, Galic, Skoblar.
SCORERS: Kadraba, Scherer (2), for Czechoslovakia; Jerkovic for
Yugoslavia.

Third Place Match

CHILE 1, YUGOSLAVIA 0 (0-0). *Santiago*

CHILE: Godoy; Eyzaguirre, Cruz, Sanchez, R., Rodriguez; Toro,
Rojas; Ramirez, Campos, Tobar, Sanchez, L.
YUGOSLAVIA: Soskic; Durkovic, Svinjarevic; Radakovic,
Markovic, Popovic; Kovacevic, Sekularac, Jerkovic, Galic,
Skoblar.
SCORER: Rojas for Chile.

Final

BRAZIL 3, CZECHOSLOVAKIA 1 (1-1). *Santiago*

BRAZIL: Gilmar; Santos, D., Mauro, Zozimo, Santos, N.; Zito,
Didì; Garrincha, Vavà, Amarildo, Zagalo.
CZECHOSLOVAKIA: Schroiff; Tichy, Novak; Pluskal, Popluhar,
Masopust; Pospichal, Scherer, Kvasniak, Kadraba, Jelinek.
SCORERS: Masopust for Czechoslovakia; Amarildo, Zito, Vavà
for Brazil.

World Cup 1966 – held in England

When he took over from Walter Winterbottom the
managership of the English national side, Alf Ramsey promised
that England would win the 1966 tournament. They did and
he did; for there had been fewer stronger examples in the
history of the game of 'the players' manager'. It was Nobby
Stiles who said it after England had beaten Germany in the
Final. 'You did it, Alf,' he cried tearfully. 'We'd have been
nothing without you.'

England had to be favourites, given home advantage, given a
successful Scandinavian tour just before the series began. On
paper they had a fine goalkeeper in Banks, a potential match-
winner in Greaves, a gifted and well-drilled defence. But in
midfield they relied on Bobby Charlton, always known as a
striker. In the event Charlton would play superbly in the semi-
final; be decisive in the Final. But those days were ahead.

Eyes also turned inevitably towards Brazil during their
Scandinavian tour. But it was clear that the great days were
passed. If Pelé was still there, threatening as ever, there were
many questions that received unsatisfactory answers. Who

would fill in for Zagalo, with his tireless and effective running?
Who was there to replace the immaculate Didì? Was Garrincha
sufficiently recovered from a car crash and a series of serious
knee operations? In fact, so strange an amalgam was the
Brazilian party between unproven young players and older
hands that they brought with them the very two defenders
they had omitted on grounds of old age four years earlier –
Bellini and Orlando.

Russia still had Yachin, still lacked the spark that makes
triumphant teams. The Italians had three stylish inside-
forwards in Mazzola, Rivera and Bulgarelli, an accomplished
goal-scoring back in the giant Facchetti. They had beaten
Argentina 3-o just before the competition opened. But they
also had a reputation for playing below form away from home.
And the Argentinians that day had fielded something of a reserve
side.

The Germans still had the indomitable Seeler up front, the
indestructible Schnellinger in defence. It was known that they
lacked a good goalkeeper, but had unearthed a fine young
attacking wing-half in Beckenbauer, still had Helmut Haller
to give guidance in midfield, and in Wolfgang Overath
possessed another midfield player of the highest skill and fierce
ability to read the patterns of a game.

The Brazilians were undoubtedly drawn in the toughest
group – against Bulgaria, Hungary and Portugal. They won
the opening game, against the first of these three, lost the
other two. Against the Bulgarians both goals came from
freekicks, a cannonball from Pelé, a 'banana' shot from
Garrincha; and Pelé spent much of the match trying to avoid
scything tackles.

The Brazilians then came across Hungary, losers to Portugal
in their first game thanks to some desperately inefficient
goalkeeping. (More than one authority thought that Hungary

would have won this competition had they been served in goal
even remotely well.) The Hungarians had Albert, one of their
heroes four years previously; they had a fine new forward in
Bene, who had played superbly in the winning 1964 Olympic
team; they had another hero from 1962 in Meszoly, always
prepared to break into attack from behind; and they had
Farkas, a deadly finisher close to goal.

Without Pelé, the Brazilians looked feeble indeed. Garrincha
looked creaky, the two elder statesmen of the defence –
Djalma Santos and Bellini – ominously static. Against fast and
tricky running, that Brazilian defence crumbled quickly. Bene
swerved and knifed through the middle after three minutes of
play to slide the ball home; and although Brazil equalized
through the young Tostao just before half-time, their goal
came against all justice.

It was in the second half that their fate was sealed. First
Albert ran through, slid the ball to Bene on the right, and
Farkas rushed in to smack home the volleyed cross – as
spectacular a goal as the competition was to see. And then
came a penalty, tucked home by Meszoly. The Liverpool crowd
rose to the Hungarians, and particularly Albert; the Brazilians
went back to camp to plan survival against Portugal.

They did for this match what they might have done earlier –
play young men capable of running for ninety minutes. Pelé
came back, clearly not fit, and was put out of the game early
on by a vicious tackle from Morais, one that failed to receive
from the too placid English referee the punishment it deserved
– expulsion. All those who saw it will never forget the sight of
Pelé, his face agonized, lying by the touchline swathed in a
blanket.

The game against Hungary had been Brazil's first defeat in a
World Cup match since 1954 – when they had been put out
in that infamous game – by the Hungarians. The Portugal

game showed that they deserved to be out. They had had no
answers to Albert, Bene and Farkas; now they had no answers
to the fast running and powerful shooting of Eusebio. It was
the famous coloured player from Mozambique who smashed
in a shot in the fourteenth minute – for Manga, the Brazilian
goalkeeper to shovel it away into the path of Simoes. A
headed goal from Eusebio, then a right-foot shot – and Brazil
(despite Rildo's second-half score) were out. They caught the
train to Euston complaining – rightly – of inefficient refereeing.
But they had proved the point that great teams are made up
of great players, that greatness is not bestowed magically from
above to those countries who feel they deserve it.

Elsewhere Argentina and West Germany came through from
group II, the former gathering a reputation for ruthlessness
that would serve to dim appreciation of their undoubted skills.
Both teams beat Switzerland and Spain, their game together
was drawn. The West Germans looked classy in a 5-0 victory
over Switzerland. They still had their own goalkeeping
problems; but the defence remained firm, the midfield
enterprising. As for Spain, they used their older players initially –
and like Brazil, came to rue their choice. When they did put
out their youngsters, it was against the Germans and too late,
despite a spirited performance.

England came through in the first group, desperately
unconvincing. Against Uruguay they were unable to pierce the
defensive barrier; against Mexico it took a superb, spectacular
shot from long-distance and Bobby Charlton to break the
deadlock; against France they looked unconvincing against a
team down to ten men for much of the game. The English
defence, however, appeared impressive; fortunate indeed to
have a goalkeeper of Banks' class in a year of so much bad
goalkeeping. The Uruguayans beat France, drew with Mexico,
to join them.

Up in the North-east it was nearly all Russia. They disposed
of North Korea in the opening game, scoring three goals in the
process; then scored just the one goal against a lethargic
Italian team bereft of Rivera's skills. As so often Italian caution
in team selection and tactics brought its just rewards. But they
still had to play North Korea – a game that should have given
them little cause for sleeplessness.

In the event, the game was as big a shock as England's defeat
at the hands of the Americans sixteen years earlier. Though the
Italians lost Bulgarelli in the thirty-fourth minute with
strained ligaments (an injury caused by his own foul tackle),
they throughout played like ghosts. Pak Doo Ik it was who
scored the only goal of the match just before half-time, and
when the final whistle came, the Middlesbrough crowd rushed
on to the pitch in joy. Who could ever forget the sight of one
enormous British sailor tucking a Korean player under each
arm and rushing round the pitch like a lunatic. As for the
Italians they went home in shame, were pelted with rotten
vegetables on arrival at Genoa airport at the dead of night.

Two of the quarter-finals remain memorable – and for totally
differing reasons. The Russians won by the odd goal in three
against the Hungarians, manifestly less imaginative, but having
in goal a Yachin instead of a Gelei; and at Sheffield the West
Germans won 4-0 against a dispirited and disorganized
Uruguayan team that had two men sent off and never really
tried to stay in the game.

London and Liverpool would see the more fascinating
matches. For their game against Argentina at Wembley,
England left out the injured Jimmy Greaves (and were perhaps
glad to do so, for his form had been disappointing) and
brought in Geoff Hurst – whose last game, against Denmark,
had been disastrously uninspiring. As so often happens in
these things, Hurst turned out to be the match-winner,

scoring the only goal of the game thirteen minutes from time;
and once forcing Roma, the Argentinian goalkeeper, to an
acrobatic windmill-like save at point-blank range.

Everything, however, came to be overshadowed in most
people's minds by the events just before half-time when Rattin,
the South Americans' captain, was sent off by the German referee,
Herr Kreitlin, for objecting to the booking of one of his team
mates. Rattin himself had been booked for a trip on Bobby
Charlton; but though there had been many nasty and cynical
Argentinian fouls, that particular one had been by no means the
worst. Later the referee claimed to have sent off Rattin 'for the look
on his face'. In the event the game was held up for eleven minutes
while Rattin refused to move, while the Argentinian coach, Juan
Carlos Lorenzo argued from the touchline, while officials tried
to get the game restarted. So the Argentinians lost the most
effective player in midfield; and there can be little doubt that
had they initially gone out to play as well as they could, the result
might have been very different. Certainly England's eleven players
made heavy work of the game in the second half against ten
opponents bent merely on destructive tactics.

After the game officials moved quickly to protect the referee
against the Argentinian reserves, who joined their colleagues to
pound on the door of the English dressing-room, to make
insinuating gestures and statements to World Cup officials.
One of their players urinated on the floor outside the English
quarters, their manager rubbed forefinger and thumb
meaningfully together, and Alf Ramsey was distressed enough
to refer to them as 'animals' in a remark that he later –
understandably grudgingly – was forced to withdraw.

England were through, the mundanity of their play masked
by events off the ball. And in the semi-finals they would meet
Portugal, winners against the North Koreans in a game as
extraordinary as that at Wembley. After their bizarre and

heart-warming achievements against the Italians, the Koreans
took on Eusebio and his men, nipping about smartly. A goal
in the first minute was a fine tonic; two more soon after and
the fancied Portuguese were three down.

That was the point at which Eusebio must have realized
that Nemesis was staring him in the face. He ran through for
one goal, smashed home a penalty after Torres had had his
legs taken from underneath him, added two further goals in
the second half. Augusto got a fifth, from a corner, and the
Koreans were finally forced out, having given vast entertainment,
having puzzled everyone as to the nature of their achievement.
Everyone knew that for months they had lived in solitary and
rigorous confinement. But the quickness with which they had
learnt made many people wonder whether future competitions
wouldn't deserve greater participation on the part of teams
drawn from those countries with little footballing tradition.

Given the magnificent way in which Lancashire – and
particularly Liverpool – had supported its games in the
competition, Liverpudlians deserved much better than they
received from the Russia–Germany semi-final, little more nor
less than a war of attrition. Sabo made a potentially vicious
tackle on Beckenbauer – only to come away limping himself;
a long-range sliding effort from Schnellinger on Chislenko
left that Russian limping. He went off for treatment, returned,
lost a ball to Held, chased the German and was rightly sent
off by Concetto Lo Bello, the famous Italian referee. Haller it
was who scored the first German goal a minute before half-time,
just after Schnellinger's tackle; and Beckenbauer curled a shot
around the Russian defensive wall for the second. Porkuian
replied for Russia, but too late. And although the Russian
manager publicly blamed Yachin for the two German goals,
the truth was that without him they might have ceded two or
three in the first twenty minutes.

The England–Portugal semi-final provided a pleasant and
enthralling contrast. It was in this game that the English really
came together to look formidable, the defence strong as ever,
Bobby Charlton stupendous in midfield and behind the attack
in a performance that must have gone a long way to earning
him the award as European Footballer of the Year. Everything
he tried, and he tried everything, came off. His swerving runs,
long passing, ferocious shooting – all were in evidence. He it
was who scored the first goal, after José Pereira had pushed
out a shot from Hunt; and just as important, every Portuguese
player he passed on the way back to the centre circle stopped
to shake his hand.

From first whistle to last the game was played at an
electrifying pace, graced by electric skills. There was the battle
between Torres and Jack Charlton, two giants in the air; that
between Stiles and Eusebio, with the heart and guts of the
former matched against the amazing skills of the latter; and
there was the battle in midfield between Charlton and the
Portuguese captain, Coluna, with his casual talent for passing,
his instinctual reading of the game. When Hurst raced through
eleven minutes from the end and cut the ball back from the
by line for Charlton to hammer in his second goal, that
seemed that. But three minutes later Jack Charlton was forced
to give away a penalty, taken and scored by Eusebio. And the
last few minutes were played out in a frenzy – Stiles making a
fine last-ditch tackle on Simoes, Banks going down brilliantly
to a vicious shot from Coluna. England were through to the
Final; and though Eusebio left the pitch in tears, comforted by
his team mates, he would have the consolation (admittedly
small) of scoring in Portugal's victory over Russia for the
third place match, and thus consolidate his position as the
tournament's leading scorer.

The Final would prove as dramatic as the changes in the

weather – now brilliant sunshine, now driving rain; certainly
the most dramatic Final that the competition has ever seen.
It was the Germans who took the lead – in the thirteenth
minute after Ray Wilson – normally so cool at fullback – had
nonchalantly headed a loose ball down to the feet of Haller,
for the German inside-forward to slide the ball past Banks. It
was a lead Germany would hold for only six minutes – until
Hurst turned in a free-kick taken too swiftly by Bobby Moore.

It was eighteen minutes into the second-half before England
took the lead. For much of the match Alan Ball had run
Schnellinger ragged – Schnellinger, thought of by many as the
best fullback in the world. Time after time Ball had forced
him away from his touchline and into the middle, where he
had been manifestly less assured. Now the small, red-haired
England 'winger' forced and took a corner. The ball came to
Hurst, who shot – only for a German defender to block and
Peters to clip the rebound past Tilkowski, the German
goalkeeper.

Pressing increasingly towards attack, the Germans were
leaving themselves vulnerable in defence. Three minutes from
what should have been the end of the game Hunt burst
through, passed too shallowly to Charlton – whose shot was
tame. And in the last minute, agonizingly, the Germans
equalized. The referee deemed Jack Charlton to have obstructed
Held (many thought the offence inverted), Emmerich drove
the kick powerfully through the England wall, and when Held
touched the ball on, Weber – the centre-half – rushed in to
score.

Thus to extra-time, with both teams exhausted apart from
Alan Ball, seemingly ready to run for many hours yet. Ten
minutes into the first period he scampered off down the
right wing and crossed precisely – for Hurst to smash a shot
against the underside of the crossbar. We can now say that it

was probably not a goal. But to establish that fact it took a
lot of people many hours of very hard work in cinema
laboratories all over the world. At the time the referee
conferred with linesman – the Russian Bakhramov – and the
most contentious goal of a World Cup final was allowed.

In the last minutes, with England having hung on bravely,
Hurst it was again who ran through a demoralized and static
German defence to slash in a fierce shot with his left foot. He
had done what no one had done before, scored a hat trick in a
Final. And England, though far from being the most stylish or
interesting team of the competition, had done what Alf
Ramsey had said they would. They would have their critics,
and many would complain about the incompetence and lack
of sensibility in much of the refereeing. But the competition
had been the best organized and best supported of any, and
England's games in semi-final and Final worthy to set with
the best in the history of the World Cup tournament.

1966 – Final Stages

Quarter-Finals

ENGLAND 1, ARGENTINA 0 (0-0). *Wembley*

ENGLAND: Banks (Leicester City); Cohen (Fulham), Wilson
(Everton); Stiles (Manchester United), Charlton, J. (Leeds
United), Moore (West Ham United); Ball (Blackpool), Hurst
(West Ham United), Charlton, R. (Manchester United), Hunt
(Liverpool), Peters (West Ham United).
ARGENTINA: Roma; Ferreiro, Perfumo, Albrecht, Marzolini;
Gonzalez, Rattin, Onega; Solari, Artime, Mas.
SCORER: Hurst for England.

T–C

WEST GERMANY 4, URUGUAY 0 (1-0). Sheffield

WEST GERMANY: Tilkowski; Hottges, Weber, Schultz,
Schnellinger; Beckenbauer, Haller, Overath; Seeler, Held,
Emmerich.
URUGUAY: Mazurkiewiez; Troche; Ubinas, Gonçalves,
Manicera, Caetano; Salva, Rocha, Silva, Cortez, Perez.
SCORERS: Held, Beckenbauer, Seeler, Haller for West Germany.

PORTUGAL 5, NORTH KOREA 3. (2-3) Everton

PORTUGAL: José Pereira; Morais, Baptista, Vicente, Hilario;
Graça, Coluna, Augusto; Eusebio, Torres, Simoes.
NORTH KOREA: Ri Chan Myung; Rim Yung Sum, Shin Yung
Kyoo, Ha Jung Wong, O Yook Kyung; Pak Seung Jin, Jon
Seung Hwi; Han Bong Jin, Pak Doo Ik, Li Dong Woon, Yang
Sung Kook.
SCORERS: Pak Seung Jin, Yang Sung Kook, Li Dong Woon for
North Korea; Eusebio 4 (2 penalties), Augusto for Portugal.

RUSSIA 2, HUNGARY 1 (1-0). Sunderland

RUSSIA: Yachin; Ponomarev, Chesternjiev, Voronin, Danilov;
Sabo, Khusainov; Chislenko, Banichevski, Malafeev, Porkujan.
HUNGARY: Gelei; Matrai; Kaposzta, Meszoly, Sipos, Szepesi;
Nagy, Albert, Rakosi; Bene, Farkas.
SCORERS: Chislenko, Porkujan for Russia; Bene for Hungary.

Semi-Finals

WEST GERMANY 2, RUSSIA 1 (1-0). Everton

WEST GERMANY: Tilkowski; Hottges, Weber, Schulz, Schnellinger;
Beckenbauer, Haller, Overath, Seeler, Held, Emmerich.

RUSSIA: Yachin; Ponomarev, Chesternjiev, Voronin, Danilov;
Sabo, Khusainov; Chislenko, Banichevski, Malafeev, Porkujan.
SCORERS: Haller, Beckenbauer for Germany; Porkujan for Russia.

ENGLAND 2, PORTUGAL 1 (1-0). *Wembley*

ENGLAND: Banks (Leicester City); Cohen (Fulham), Wilson
(Everton); Stiles (Manchester United), Charlton, J. (Leeds
United), Moore (West Ham United); Ball (Blackpool), Hurst
(West Ham United), Charlton, R. (Manchester United), Hunt
(Liverpool), Peters (West Ham United).
PORTUGAL: José Pereira; Festa, Baptista, Carlos, Hilario; Graça,
Coluna, Augusto; Eusebio, Torres, Simoes.
SCORERS: Charlton, R. (2) for England; Eusebio (penalty) for
Portugal.

Third Place Match

PORTUGAL 2, RUSSIA 1 (1-1). *Wembley*

PORTUGAL: José Pereira; Festa, Baptista, Carlos, Hilario; Graça,
Coluna, Augusto; Eusebio, Torres, Simoes.
RUSSIA: Yachin; Ponomarev, Khurtsilava, Korneev, Danilov;
Voronin, Sichinava; Metreveli, Malafeev, Banichevski,
Serebrianikov.
SCORERS: Eusebio (penalty), Torres for Portugal; Malafeev for
Russia.

Final

ENGLAND 4, WEST GERMANY 2 (1-1) (2-2) after extra time.
Wembley

ENGLAND: Banks; Cohen, Wilson; Stiles, Charlton, J., Moore;
Ball, Hurst, Charlton, R., Hunt, Peters.
WEST GERMANY: Tilkowski; Hottges, Schulz; Weber,
Schnellinger, Haller; Beckenbauer, Overath, Seeler, Held,
Emmerich.
SCORERS: Hurst (3), Peters for England; Haller, Weber for
Germany.

World Cup 1970 – held in Mexico

Given that the tournament tended to be played alternately in
Europe and South America, it was inevitable that Mexico
would be a venue sooner or later. For many, however, the
'later' would have been preferable. The 1968 Olympiad had
shown precisely and agonizingly the problems thrown up in
expecting top-class athletes to compete at high altitudes. And
few parts of central Mexico were at less than 6–7,000 feet above
sea level. The nonchalant could at least pretend that it made
life more interesting.

What could have been prevented – and wasn't – was the
callous selling-out of the tournament to financial interests. Too
many games were played in noonday heat – merely to satisfy
European television companies eager to televise games at peak
viewing times. England, for example, played their vital group
match against Brazil at noon, in temperatures of nearly 100
degrees and there was barely an England player who had not
lost eight or ten pounds in weight as a result of dehydration.

England's preparations had been thorough enough. The

team arrived in Mexico well before the tournament started;
good accommodation had been found; supplies of food and
drink had been flown out (though the Mexican customs
officials appeared un-cooperative at first); the players were
even supplied with reading material by Coronet Books, one of
the country's leading paperback publishing firms. Leaving
Mexico for a short tour, England won handsome victories
over Columbia and Ecuador, the defence seemingly as
ungenerous as it had been in 1966.

It was after the second of these games, as the team stopped
off in Bagota on the way back to Mexico that Bobby Moore,
the English captain, was absurdly accused of having stolen a
bracelet from a hotel jewellers. Much has been written about
this extraordinary incident, that would last for nearly two years,
until the 'charges' were finally dropped. The important point
to underline is Moore's amazing coolness during the whole
affair. In a situation where many players might have cracked
under the nervous strain imposed by being unable to fly back
to Mexico with the rest of the team, of having to remain in
a state of semi-solitary confinement while the matter was
tentatively cleared up Moore was simply magnificent. Within
days he was to go out and prove to the world that, as in 1966,
he remained the best defensive wing-half in modern football.

If England had Moore, then Brazil still had Pelé. The Brazilians
had taken, only months before the Finals, the extraordinary step
of sacking their manager, the bubbling Joao Saldanha, and
replacing him with Mario Zagalo, one of the heroes of 1958 and
1962. No one doubted the Brazilian talent. If they had a goalkeeper
of laughable mediocrity in Felix, if their defence seemed
unsound – then they had Gerson in midfield and up front
Jairzinho and Tostao. The latter had recently undergone eye
surgery, but was known to be a formidable foil to Pelé. The
first few games would tell all about Brazil.

The West Germans were there also, eager for the chance to
revenge their defeat at the hands of the English four years
previously. The bulk of that side remained, they had two
incisive wingers in Grabowski and Libuda, a 'new' goalkeeper
in Maier, one of the best of the tournament. And that is not
meant disparagingly. One of the many contrasts between the
1966 competition and that to be held in Mexico would be the
overall improvement in goalkeeping standards. Banks (England),
Kavazashvili (Russia), Piot (Belgium), Calderon (Mexico),
Albertosi (Italy) and Mazurkiewicz (Uruguay) – all, with
Maier, kept goal well in conditions that were far from helpful,
ones in which the ball moved fast through the rarefied air,
swerving and dipping unexpectedly, ones in which the
brightness of the light put a premium on good judgement.
We might note here that the fearsome Gerd Muller, who
would score most goals in the tournament, came to face only
two of the above-mentioned, when Germany played their
semi-final against Italy and their final game against Uruguay.

The Italians came strangely, having qualified with some ease
against East Germany and Wales in their preliminary group.
In Riva they had a striker of renown, his left foot a terrifying
weapon when given the chance to exercise itself. But too often
Riva's brilliant goals had camouflaged weaknesses in the defence,
lack of understanding in midfield. Mazzola was there for the
second time, Rivera for the third – both players of high
technical accomplishment, and supposedly unable to play
together. The Italians decided in favour of the *staffeta*, a system
whereby Mazzola would play the first half of each game, Rivera
the second. The latter found it unacceptable, said so loudly,
was nearly sent home as punishment, stayed, and in two
games at least, would prove that he is one of the world's great
intuitive players.

The Russians looked solid as ever, with Kavazashvili a

worthy successor in goal to the great Yachin, and Shesternev
a sweeper little behind Bobby Moore in terms of technical
expertise and tactical acumen. They had an interesting young
striker in Bishovets, but would play a type of football that
lacked genuine inventiveness. Uruguay were another team
strong on paper, again served brilliantly in goal (by
Mazurkiewicz, one of the very small clutch of good
goalkeepers four years previously), and with some terrifyingly
robust defenders. One remembers particularly Montero
Castillo in the centre of the defence, Ubinas and Ancheta
elsewhere. And the joker in the pack had to be Peru, coached
for the tournament by Didì, the Brazilian ex-player and
perennial hero of 1954, 1958 and 1962. It was known that
they had some forwards of dazzling technical gifts, but did
they have a team, could they put together a game?

Generally speaking those teams that were expected to come
through, came through. The first game of the first group –
and the tournament – was that between Mexico (the hosts)
and Russia. A goalless draw, as with its 1966 counterpart,
sounded an ominous warning. But Belgium played some light,
waltzing football to beat El Salvador the following day; and
when they came to meet Russia, deserved better than the 4-1
defeat that they allowed to be inflicted upon them. Bishovets
scored two of those goals, Shesternev marshalled the defence
superbly; and it was one of those days when the Russians
showed the world just what they could do when prepared to
cast off thoughts of weighty preparation and over-drilled
tactics. And in the final game of the group, the Mexicans went
through against the Belgians 1-0, thanks to a hotly disputed
penalty decision, one that seemed to have been not
uninfluenced by the frenzy of a vast home crowd. Mexico,
unconvincingly, and Russia through, then, from that group.

Group II looked good for both Italy and Uruguay. Israel

looked too raw, Sweden – despite the presence of one or two
players of high talent, such as Kindvall and Grahn, who
played their club football outside Sweden – lacked strength in
depth. They it was who first faced Italy, going down to a drive
from some long range delivered by the Italian midfield player,
Domenghini, who throughout the tournament would play with
a ubiquity that perilously ignored the heat of the sun and the
rarity of the air. The Uruguayans scraped through 2-0 against
Israel, more importantly lost Pedro Rocha, their midfield
general after only a few minutes of play. It was an injury that
would force the South American team even further back on to
their defensive and uncompromising heels, for Rocha would
take no further part in the tournament.

The next match brought these two teams together into a
goalless draw, with both sets of players full of hostility (both
masked and overt). Riva was to claim that from the first
Uruguayan defenders had spat at him whenever they were
close; which did not excuse his lethargy. More dreary football
was to follow, and the results continued to prove evidence
of the essentially defensive attitudes that permeated group
matches. The Swedes beat the Uruguayans, who went through
on a marginally better goal average; and the Italians got
through with two goalless draws and that one win. Top of the
group with only one goal in three matches: that, surely,
couldn't be the stuff of which world champions were made?

Group III was, indubitably, the toughest on paper; and
certainly the matches from that group provided some of the
most fascinating football. If the English won their first game
against Rumania, they did so with some lack of ease, thanks
to a goal from Geoff Hurst in the seventieth minute, and
despite some sadistic tackling by the Rumanian defenders, a
certain Mocanu in particular. If the Brazilians appeared to
thrash the Czechs 4-1, it must be remembered that Petras

scored the first goal of the match for Czechoslovakia, that they were served with some indifferent goalkeeping, that the third Brazilian goal (scored by Jairzinho) looked suspiciously offside. But Pelé was on superb form, scored a goal; Rivellino put another in from a swerving free-kick; Jairzinho scored again, always threatened when he had possession; and Gerson in midfield sprayed accurate passes around with high panache, underlining the thought that so many of the world's finest distributors have been players whose athleticism was far from robust. Gerson, for example, is something of a one-paced player (and that pace never faster than slow-medium) who is a compulsive cigarette smoker. Hardly the stuff of which the textbook heroes are made, but a player of great influence.

Too many people – and particularly in England – have tended to overlook the fact of Gerson's absence when England came to play Brazil. That is not to say that England didn't play thoroughly well, that they did not suggest themselves as one of the two or three best teams of the tournament during that game. It was a classic, worthy to enter the Pantheon of brilliant World Cup games. The English had gone to Mexico in the rôle of villains, with too many people disgruntled as to the manner of their victory four years earlier; and this animosity was to manifest itself at every turn. The night before the Brazil game a crowd several thousand strong milled round the Hilton Hotel, where they were staying, and contrived to make enough noise to prevent the players getting any sleep. Many admitted afterwards that they had for long minutes and hours simply stood by the windows of their rooms, staring at the crowd below, and at the inability of the Mexican police to deal with the problem.

They then went out at midday, in scorching heat that approached 100 degrees of Fahrenheit and played Brazil off the pitch for long stretches of the game. Mullery played

brilliantly, policing Pelé with scrupulous toughness. True,
Pelé got away from him in the early minutes of the game after
Jairzinho had rounded Cooper on England's left and smacked
across a perfect centre; up went Pelé, down came the ball, and
down also came Gordon Banks to scoop the ball up with his
right wrist – a save that must rank with the very best in the
history of the World Cup tournament. Otherwise Pelé was kept
moderately quiet; and Moore at the heart of the defence gave
further evidence that he was the best defensive player in the
world, his timing of the tackle precise, his reading of the game
astute, his distribution imaginative.

The only goal of the match (perfect evidence that goals in
themselves do not exciting football make) came after fourteen
minutes of the second half, after Tostao had teased the left of the
English defence and slid the ball across goal for Jairzinho to
score. The truth was, however, that if Banks was forced to at least
three other saves of high quality, England were given, and missed,
a plenitude of chances at the other end. Ball hit the bar, missed
another good chance; Astle blazed wide after being put into an
attractive position; Hurst might have had a goal, but shot
feebly at the crucial moment. If the style is the man, then the
style must also be the game; and yet again we were left to ponder
that one of the essential weaknesses of the English game was its
lack of high technical accomplishment – where the world's best
strikers would snap up chances with glee, too often English
forwards had not the basic 'killer' instinct that comes hand in
hand (or foot to foot) with technical prowess.

The Brazilians went on to beat the Rumanians, again despite
the deprivation of Gerson; and, on this occasion, that of
Rivellino. England drafted in a handful of 'reserves' for the
game against the Czechs, played badly, won through a disputed
penalty; and joined Brazil in the quarter-finals.

In group IV were the mysterious Peruvians. In their first

game, they fell behind to Bulgaria, conceded two goals from
set pieces; and then in the second half turned on their skills.
Many were quick to compare them with the Brazilians in their
flamboyance, their brilliant control. They had a sturdy midfield
player in Chumpitaz, some imaginative forwards in Gallardo,
Sotil, Cubillas and Baylon; and in the space of twenty minutes
turned the two-goal deficit into a 3-2 score that would last
until the game's finish.

That would prove to be the decisive game in the group. For
although they fared poorly against Morocco in their first
match, the West Germans seemed certainties for qualification;
a thought that was reinforced when they came to play the
Bulgarians in turn. Though the East Europeans scored first
through Nikodimov (following a free kick), the Germans ran
in five goals, three of them going to Muller. Libuda was on
venomous form on their right, Muller and Seeler brave and
energetic in the middle. In fact Muller would score another
hat trick when the Germans came to meet Peru a few days
later, marching firmly along the road that would make him
the tournament's highest scorer. Despite that 3-1 defeat, Peru
would qualify.

No goal Muller scored in the competition was, however, more
important than that he slashed home in the quarter-final tie that
followed, when the Germans were drawn against England. It was
a game England could, and should, have won. For a team of
their defensive prowess to lead by two clear goals and eventually
lose by the odd score in five was remarkable. It is too easy to
blame Peter Bonetti, drafted into the goalkeeping position
after Banks had been forced to withdraw with a stomach
complaint of mysterious origin. Banks may well have saved
two of the three German goals to be scored; but there were
other, better reasons to explain the collapse.

England's lead came through Mullery – racing through to

exchange passes with Lee, sliding the ball out to Newton on the
right, smashing home the perfect cross; and Peters – knocking
in another fine cross from Newton. That left England two up
after five minutes of the second half, and seemingly set for a
good win. And then came the substitutions – Grabowski on
for Libuda; Bell and Hunter on for Charlton and Peters –
that were to prove decisive. While Charlton remained,
Beckenbauer, his policeman, stayed quiet; without further
patrolling duties, Beckenbauer cut loose, scored the first,
important, German goal. Where Cooper had controlled Libuda
on the left, he now found Grabowski irrepressible. Although
Hurst nearly made the score 3-1 with a fine low header, it was
the Germans who came through, Seeler backheading a long
cross from Schnellinger.

As in the 1966 Final, the game between the two countries
entered extra time, with the crowd noisily pro-German, and
England's defence looking increasingly tired. Hurst scored – to
be given, mysteriously, offside. And then came the deciding
goal – Grabowski winning control on the right, punting over
a cross, which Muller tucked away as the ball was nodded
down to him. England were out of the competition, after
having controlled vast stretches of their games against Brazil
and West Germany, after having suggested themselves strongly
as possible opposition for Brazil in the Final.

Through into the semi-finals with Germany would go Italy,
Brazil and Uruguay. The last won through in the final moments
of extra time in a hard game against the Russians, and with a
hotly disputed goal into the bargain. But the Russians had
missed too many chances to have reason for bitter complaint.

Brazil went through, now with both Rivelino and Gerson
back in the side, and at the expense of Peru to the tune of 4-2.
Gallardo scored two goals for the entertaining Peruvians, but
they were up against a side that knew their own footballing

language and were more adept practitioners.

And Italy went through, stuttering for much of their game against Mexico, until Gianni Rivera made his appearance at the start of the second half and suggested openings for his compatriots. Riva scored twice, delighting those who knew his prowess and were still waiting patiently for evidence of its existence; and there was a goal from Rivera himself, nice ammunition for those who felt that Italy were squandering his exquisite talents, that there should always have been a place for him in that team, with or without the brave and resourceful Sandro Mazzola.

The semi-final draw – Brazil against Uruguay, Italy against West Germany – promised, and delivered, much. The first of these games pitted the resource of the Brazilian midfield and attack against the misanthropy of the Uruguayan defence, with its squad of muscular central defenders. In the event, it was Uruguay who scored first, through Cubilla (as opposed to Cubillas, the Peruvian); and though Brazil equalized just before half time through Clodoaldo, the important second goal did not materialize until fourteen minutes before the end, when Jairzinho danced past three defenders on the right and drove the ball home from a sharp angle. A goal from Rivelino in the last seconds of the game gave the scoreline a lopsided quality that was grossly unfair to the courage and ingenuity of much of the Uruguayan play, still deprived of the skills of the injured – and potentially influential – Pedro Rocha.

But Italy against West Germany – that was really something of a collector's item. It was an interesting comment on the Italian footballing mentality that after a game of thrilling interest, despite the fact that their team was victorious, many Italian commentators would dismiss it as being something of a circus turn on the grounds that neither of the two defences was good enough. In fact, Italy created much of their good fortune

early in the game when a bad tackle by Bertini left the elegant
Beckenbauer with an injured arm. He would play much of the
game at strolling pace and in some pain, his arm strapped to
his chest.

The Italians took the lead after only seven minutes,
Boninsegna clearing Riva out of his way to plant a left-footed
shot firmly past Maier. Given the Italian penchant for defensive
expertise, the Germans must have known that they had a titanic
struggle on their hands, and well though they played against
the cautious Italians in the second half, too many chances went
begging. Indeed it was not until the third minute of injury
time that Schnellinger, the German sweeper (and ironically he
served brilliantly in that rôle at club level for A.C. Milan),
came forward to slide the ball home after Grabowski had
crossed from the left.

Into extra-time, and on came the nervousness and the
mistakes. The Germans went ahead after five minutes through
Muller; Burgnich came up to knock in Rivera's free kick; Riva
scored a fine goal with that formidable left foot of his – and
the first period of extra-time ended with Italy leading 3-2.
The Italians were pulled back again soon after the resumption
of play, when Muller dived low to head home; and then came
the decisive goal, with the talented Boninsegna taking the ball
out to the left, leaving his opponent Schulz on his bottom,
and crossing for Gianni Rivera to drive the ball precisely into
goal. Once again Rivera had missed the first forty-five minutes;
once again he had been decisive in the later stages of a game.
The Italians were through, not remotely the second best side
in the tournament, but undoubtedly one of high technical
accomplishment, and in that semi-final game, having given the
lie to those detractors eager to claim that Italian teams always
lack fire and spirit.

In the play-off for third place the Germans did what the

Italians had failed to do – and beat Uruguay. They did so with
a fine goal scored by Overath after a thrilling movement that
involved Libuda, Muller and Seeler. There was entertaining
action at both ends, with Mazurkiewicz and Walter (the young
German goalkeeper) both being forced to fine saves. But a
match of technical adroitness could not raise the crowd –
which, like the televised world, awaited the Final itself.

Brazil won it, and won it handsomely. They did so with
football of assured fluency, they did it by underlining
brilliantly, and against the master exponents of defensive
football, all the old clichés about attack being the best means
of defence. Of the Italians Sandro Mazzola covered vast tracts
of ground, played with authority and spirit; Boninsegna
showed what a dangerous striker he could be, given even
a few metres of space; Facchetti strove manfully against
Jairzinho. But much of the marking was sloppy on the one
hand, crude on the other; and there was about the team as
a whole a curious refusal to play with any real vestige of
self-confidence.

It was, fittingly, Pelé who gave the Brazilians the lead after
eighteen minutes, heading down Rivelino's cross; if the great
man had a comparatively human game, then his presence and
brilliance had given the tournament as a whole a fine streak of
class. And no one looked more bemused than he when the
Italians equalized a few minutes before half-time through
Boninsegna and after a silly back-pass by Clodoaldo had left
Felix stranded outside the Brazilian goal.

That was delusion indeed, for in the second half, the
Brazilians made heavy amends. Gerson, who throughout
played with a majesty that capitalized on the failure of the
Italian midfield, was the scorer of the second of the four
Brazilian goals, his left foot curling in a fine shot from
distance. Jairzinho it was who scored the third, slipping in a

pass from Pelé and setting a new record by virtue of having
scored in all six of the games in which he had played; and the
Italians were a thoroughly demoralized side by the time Carlos
Alberto came through down the right touchline to crash the
ball in after an exquisitely weighted pass from Pelé had put
him through in the last few minutes of the game.

The Italians brought on Juliano for the ineffectual Bertini;
with six minutes to go, bizarrely substituted Rivera for
Boninsegna – a move that was staggering in its lack of logic.
Had Rivera appeared earlier, in place of the tired Domenghini,
one might have seen the point, he might have effected
something of a rescue. But the ship had been truly sunk;
despite their appearance in the Final the Italians would go
home and indulge in the most Macchiavellian post-mortems.
And by virtue of their third victory, the Brazilians would
appropriate the Jules Rimet trophy.

It was a popular victory, a welcome evidence that attacking
football and intuitive genius still had their place in a
footballing world obsessed by 'work-rate' and (often) skill-less
hard running. Winning the tournament in 1966 England had
conceded only three goals, scored eleven. Four years later, the
Brazilians had triumphed by conceding seven goals and scoring
nineteen. Either England or West Germany – not to mention
Uruguay – might have made of the Final more than did the
Italians. And it remained true (as it may always remain true)
that some of the refereeing left much to be desired. But
Ferenc Puskas, and many other great stars of the past, would
have approved. The football of the Brazilians was many
miles removed from the 'war' that people had gloomily
forecast as being the only result of international competition.
Above all, the Brazilians made the thing look enjoyable, had
helped to restore that enthusiasm without which sport in any
form will wither away. More chants of 'samba', and the spectacle

of the greatest player of that, or any, generation – Pelé – being
raised aloft by delighted Brazilian fans.

1970 – Final Stages
Quarter-Finals

WEST GERMANY 3, ENGLAND 2 (0-1) (2-2) after extra time.
Leon

WEST GERMANY: Maier; Schnellinger, Vogts, Fichtel, Hottges
(Schulz); Beckenbauer, Overath, Seeler; Libuda (Grabowski),
Muller, Loehr.
ENGLAND: Bonetti (Chelsea); Newton (Everton); Cooper
(Leeds United); Mullery (Spurs), Labone (Everton), Moore
(West Ham United); Lee (Manchester City), Ball (Everton),
Hurst (West Ham United), Charlton (Manchester United)
[Bell (Manchester City)], Peters (Spurs) [Hunter (Leeds
United)].
SCORERS: Mullery, Peters for England; Beckenbauer, Seeler,
Muller for West Germany.

BRAZIL 4, PERU 2 (2-1). *Guadalajara*
BRAZIL: Felix; Carlos Alberto, Brito, Piazza, Marco Antonio;
Clodoaldo, Gerson (Paulo Cesar); Jairzinho (Roberto), Tostao,
Pelé, Rivelino.
PERU: Rubiños; Campos, Fernandez, Chumpitaz, Fuentes;
Mifflin, Challe; Baylon (Sotil), Perico Leon (Eladio Reyes),
Cubillas, Gallardo.
SCORERS: Rivelino, Tostao (2), Jairzinho for Brazil; Gallardo,
Cubillas for Peru.

ITALY 4, MEXICO 1 (1-1). *Toluca*
ITALY: Albertosi; Burgnich, Cera, Rosato, Facchetti; Bertini,
Mazzola (Rivera), De Sisti; Domenghini (Gori), Boninsegna, Riva.

MEXICO: Calderon; Vantolra, Pena, Guzman, Perez; Gonzales
(Borja), Pulido, Munguia (Diaz); Valdivia, Fragoso, Padilla.
SCORERS: Domenghini, Riva (2), Rivera for Italy; Gonzalez for
Mexico.

URUGUAY 1, RUSSIA 0 (0-0) after extra time. *Mexico*

URUGUAY: Mazurkiewicz; Ubinas, Ancheta, Matosas, Mujica;
Maneiro, Cortes, Montero Castillo; Cubilla, Fontes (Gomez),
Morales (Esparrago).
RUSSIA: Kavazashvili; Dzodzuashvili, Afonin, Khurtsilava
(Logofet), Chesternijev; Muntijan, Asatiani (Kiselev),
Kaplichni; Evriuzhkinzin, Bychevetz, Khmelnitzki.
SCORER: Esparrago for Uruguay.

Semi-Finals

ITALY 4, WEST GERMANY 3 (1-0) (1-1) after extra time.
Mexico City

ITALY: Albertosi; Cera; Burgnich, Bertini, Rosato, (Poletti)
Facchetti; Domenghini, Mazzola (Rivera), De Sisti;
Boninsegna, Riva.
WEST GERMANY: Maier; Schnellinger; Vogts, Schulz,
Beckenbauer, Patzke; Seeler, Overath; Grabowski, Muller,
Loehr (Libuda.)
SCORERS: Boninsenga, Burgnich, Riva, Rivera, for Italy;
Schnellinger, Muller (2) for West Germany.

BRAZIL, 3 URUGUAY 1 (1-1). *Guadalajara*

BRAZIL: Felix; Carlos Alberto, Brito, Piazza, Everaldo;
Clodoaldo, Gerson; Jairzinho, Tostao, Pelé, Rivelino.

URUGUAY: Mazurkiewicz; Ubinas, Ancheta, Matosas, Mujica;
Montero Castillo, Cortes, Fontes; Cubilla, Maneiro
(Esparrago), Morales.
SCORERS: Cubilla for Uruguay; Clodoaldo, Jairzinho, Rivelino
for Brazil.

Third Place Match

WEST GERMANY 1, URUGUAY 0 (1-0). *Mexico City*

WEST GERMANY: Walter, Schnellinger (Lorenz); Patzke,
Fichtel, Weber, Vogts; Seeler, Overath; Libuda (Loehr),
Muller, Held.
URUGUAY: Mazurkiewicz; Ubinas, Ancheta, Matosas Mujica;
Montero Castillo, Cortes, Fontes, (Sandoval); Cubilla, Maneiro
(Esparrago), Morales.
SCORER: Overath for West Germany.

Final

BRAZIL 4, ITALY 1 (1-1). *Mexico City*

BRAZIL: Felix; Carlos Alberto, Brito, Piazza, Everaldo;
Clodoaldo, Gerson; Jairzinho, Tostao, Pelé, Rivelino.
ITALY: Albertosi; Cera; Burgnich, Bertini, (Juliano), Rosato,
Facchetti; Domenghini, Mazzola, De Sisti; Boninsegna (Rivera),
Riva.
SCORERS: Pelé, Gerson, Jairzinho, Carlos Alberto for Brazil;
Boninsegna for Italy.

3 FOOTBALL ROUND THE WORLD

It must be obvious that football is played to the same rules, and also played to the same sort of regulations throughout the world. But rules are only the framework of the game, and what lies between that framework varies considerably in appeal, style and character from continent to continent, from country to country. As no two painters will put on to canvas completely similar ideas, so no two teams play exactly the same when it comes to international competition.

There are some similarities, of course. Climate is important. From those countries used to wet weather that turns pitches into heavy masses, it is optimism indeed to expect to see brilliant ball control. The premium will tend to be in strength, in close teamwork, in sophisticated tactics. Those countries used to heat, conversely, often produce ball-juggling players of extraordinary reflex. Go to Brazil and you will see at any time of day on the famous Copacabana beach outside Rio thousands of youngsters playing happily for hours under the hot sun; go to Italy or Spain or Portugal and you will see the same sort of skills displayed at every turn.

The process becomes self-perpetuating, naturally; so that young players take to the paths trod by their successful elders. But the styles do – to a certain extent – reflect national characteristics and attitudes. Foreign visitors to Britain often find very amusing our obsession with queues – and there is much of the queue mentality about British football. The Italians have a reputation for being something of a peacock nation – all noise and bustle and beauty; and this is reflected in their football, along with the very fundamental caution of the Italian character. Russian teams of the past twenty years epitomized the heaviness of the national political character –

drilled to perfection, their players have seldom been encouraged
to express their individual skills, instead are all bound to act
within the framework of a heavily regimented squad of players.
The West Germans have that same penchant for regimentation –
but allow their players freedom to spread their talents. The
performances of the West German team in winning the
European Nations Cup of 1972 perfectly underlined the great
strength of West German football.

   Of course, that achievement underlined something else –
that great teams are formed when there is within them a
nucleus of truly great players. Just looking at some of the
better performances since the war in club and international
terms we can see this point clearly underlined. The dazzling
Hungarians in the early Fifties had Puskas, Boszik, Kocsis,
Hidegkuti and Grosics; the Real Madrid club side that swept
off with the European Cup five years running had the
incomparable Gento and Di Stefano throughout and at times
players such as Kopa, Puskas, Rial and Del Sol; the Brazilians
of 1958 and 1962 had Gilmar in goal, forwards such as Pelé,
Didì and Garrincha – not to mention the ubiquitous Zagalo;
the 1966 England team had two fine fullbacks in Wilson and
Cohen, a fine goalkeeper in Banks, a peerless defender in Bobby
Moore and in Bobby Charlton a midfield player of enormous
technical accomplishment; and the present West German
team have players such as Beckenbauer, Netzer, Muller, Vogts,
Overath and Breitner.

   If the differences between teams and teams, players and
players, countries and countries are sometimes acute, then one
factor has come, unhappily, to weld together every type of
football – the need for success and its corollary, the need to
make money. Football is a wealthy sport because it is a fine
sport and because it attracts large numbers of people prepared
to pay fair sums of money to watch it being played. But there

are different types of success. While Hungary dazzled the
footballing world in the early Fifties and Real Madrid and
Brazil later in that decade, many coaches tried to copy their
styles of play – to go out with teams bent on fluent attacking
football. While Internazionale of Milan carried much before
them during the Sixties using an ultra-defensive system, while
the 1966 World Cup was won by a team renowned for its
defensive solidity rather than its attacking flair – then the
footballing world, in imitation, slunk back into its shell. Then
came the triumph of the Brazilians in 1970, the emergence of
a fine West German national team, the victories of Ajax of
Amsterdam in European club football – and immediately the
cry was for 'total football'. The phrase means what it says –
and begins with the ability of strong defenders to play with
genuine skill, fine ball-control, tactical appreciation. It is
certainly not new as a theory. During the 1950's, in his famous
book *Soccer Revolution*, Willy Meisl propounded the theory of 'the
Whirl' – whereby defenders would attack, attackers would
defend; a system that would encourage higher skills on the
part of all players, not merely those concerned with the
business of attack. But it is only recently that we have had
practical evidence that Meisl's wishes may come true.

That, then, is the hope – the hope that we shall this summer
see the sort of football that maintains its national characteristics
at base but is nevertheless conscious of the fundamentals of
the game – that skill is important in ensuring victory, that
hard work and teamwork in themselves are only the basis of
a good squad. Perhaps by looking at the historical character
of some of the world's best international teams we can understand
one aspect of the thing – the other remains in the hands of the
players, or of God.

Argentina

Football was introduced there at the end of the last century by
British residents of Buenos Aires; but it was not until the
arrival (in large numbers) of Italian immigrants that the game
really took hold of the public imagination, early this century.
Indeed the parent has often been harsh on the child – for during
both the Thirties and the Fifties wealthy Italian clubs raided
the Argentinian football market and carried off many great
stars. Traditionally skilful and pleasing, local football has
degenerated in recent years into cynical violence, possibly a
reflection of the political malaise that has dogged the country
since Peron collapsed. Violence among players and fans alike
has made many wonder whether Argentina will be allowed to
play host to the 1978 edition of the World Cup, as is planned
at the moment.

World Cup achievement:

1930 – Second
1934 – Beaten in first round of finals
1938 – Did not enter
1950 – Did not enter
1954 – Failed to qualify
1958 – Last in group
1962 – Third in group
1966 – Quarter-finalists
1970 – Failed to qualify

Brazil

Introduced by Britons, football in Brazil was truly developed by a Hungarian, Dori Kurschner, who got over the secret of teamwork and tactics to add to natural flair. A country that has produced an army of magnificently talented players – ball-jugglers of genius, intuitive in their grasp of how the game should be played. Chief among these have been Leonidas – who named himself after a Greek hero, and played with bright brilliance before the war, famed the world over for his aerial bicycle kick; and since the war, Pelé – with his extraordinarily elastic movements and a sense of ball-control worthy of a conjurer. Popular wherever they play, the Brazilians always give the impression of enjoying the game, of still being able to think of it in artistic terms, not merely monetary ones. This despite the enormous wealth that accrues to leading players.

World Cup achievement:

1930 – Second in qualifying pool
1934 – Beaten in first qualifying round
1938 – Semi-finalists, third
1950 – Finalists, second
1954 – Quarter-finalists
1958 – Winners
1962 – Winners
1966 – Third in qualifying group
1970 – Winners

Bulgaria

The Bulgarian football association was founded in 1923, but it
was only after the war that the country's footballing prowess
came to be recognized overseas. The players are well drilled,
strong and often possess exceptional powers of ball control.
Among recent stars for the Bulgarian national side was Georgi
Asparoukhov, tragically killed in an automobile accident in
1971 – a tall, powerful centre-forward who began life as a
volleyball player. Much of the club football since the war has
been dominated by the Army side CDNA (Centralen Dom
Narodny Arme) which won the league title nine times running
between 1954 and 1962. Three times the Bulgarians have
reached the finals of a World Cup Tournament, and have yet
to win a game. The Olympics have been more kind.

World Cup achievement:

1958 – Failed to qualify for finals
1962 – Last in qualifying pool
1966 – Last in qualifying pool
1970 – Third in qualifying pool

England

The Football Association was formed in 1863, the F.A. Cup
introduced in 1871.

  With regard to international football, England withdrew
from FIFA in 1928 after having made a stand about the
professionalism that existed inside the officially amateur
Olympic football tournaments. They would remain outside
until after the 1939-45 war; and in 1938 refused an invitation
to take part in the World Cup finals being played that year in
France. The characteristics of the game are its great vigour, its
professionalism, its comparative lack of hysteria. These ensure
that when great players are thrown up, they are of genuine
world class. And in recent years Alf Ramsey has given back to
the international team much of the self-respect that it had
before and just after the war. Other countries have caught up
in terms of organization, but England are always thought of as
the hardest of all international teams to beat.

World Cup achievement:

1950 – Second in qualifying group
1954 – Quarter-finalists
1958 – Lost group play-off
1962 – Quarter-finalists
1966 – Winners
1970 – Quarter-finalists

Holland

Strange to say that while Dutch club football has prospered
over the past few years, the last time the international side
made an appearance in a World Cup finals was in 1938.
Although Dutch football came quickly on to the scene at the
beginning of the century – and under the influence of British
coaches – professionalism was a long time in the coming.
Since the war there have been two distinct periods – up to
1956, when regional leagues were played, using amateur
players; and since, particularly in the last ten years, when the
league has been dominated by Ajax of Amsterdam and
Feyenoord of Rotterdam. Both have won the European Cup
and the World Cup championship; and there are few teams
who can live with them. PSV Eindhoven have the backing of
the Philips electrical works; FC Twente have made some
progress. But the thing remains something of a two-horse race.
Perhaps it is this that is partly responsible for the growth in
Holland of the 'total football' that people talk about. Both
Ajax and Feyenoord often win games by large margins; and
the feeling of security that results must give their players the
self-confidence to go out and express themselves freely in
terms of footballing skills.

World Cup achievement:

1934 – Lost in first round
1938 – Lost in first round

Italy

Although the game was introduced to Italy by a Torinese
businessman, Eduardo Bosio (who had visited England and
been taken by the game), Genoa Football and Cricket Club was
the first of the great clubs; and English entrepreneurs had
much to do with its growth.

But the key figure in the earliest years of the game in Italy
was undoubtedly Vittorio Pozzo – an amazing man who was
in charge of the Italian team that played in the 1912 Olympiad
in Stockholm, and who would manage the Italian national
team as late as 1948 (when a brilliant England team travelled
to Turin and beat the fancied Italians 4-0). Pozzo it was who,
as a student in England before the Great War, learned much
from English football and took the lessons back to Italy – with
enough success to see his teams twice win the World Cup.

Since the war Italian football has been crazy in the extreme.
The amount of money paid to players has placed a premium
upon the art of defence, upon not losing matches, rather than
winning them. And with wealth has come semi-monopoly. It
is the great teams of the north (Juventus and Torino of Turin;
A.C. Milan and Internazionale of Milan) who have dominated
the league. Only four times has that monopoly been broken;
twice by Fiorentina, once by Bologna, once by Cagliari – who
had Luigi Riva in their forward line and a defence that gave
away only eleven goals in thirty matches in 1969-70. Italy
has also been the leading country in Europe for importation
of foreign players, and during the Fifties, the Italian league
came close to resembling a United Nations sub-committee.

Technically brilliant, tactically shrewd, Italian players lead
strange lives, subjected at all times to ritiro – the system
whereby they are grouped together in training camps for a

couple of days before and after each match. Many earn vast
sums of money per annum (the leading players anything up to
£60,000) and the majority much more than their British
counterparts. Given the predominance of the Big Four clubs,
little wonder, then, that the Italian record in European club
competition is so good.

World Cup achievement:

1934 – Winners
1938 – Winners
1950 – Second in group
1954 – Lost play-off for quarter-final place
1958 – Failed to qualify
1962 – Third in group
1966 – Third in group
1970 – Finalists, second

Mexico

The Mexican association was founded in 1927, the country
took part in the World Cup finals three years later – and have
always been in evidence when World Cup tournaments are
mentioned, thanks to the weakness of many of the teams in
their part of the world. But they have often produced some
players of talent, including Carbajal, a goalkeeper who would
play in five sets of finals between 1950 and 1966; and
Enrique Borja, a centre-forward with fine control and a fierce
shot in addition to good heading power.

World Cup achievement:

1930 – Last in group
1934 – Did not compete
1938 – Did not compete
1950 – Last in group
1954 – Last in group
1958 – Last in group
1962 – Third in group
1966 – Third in group
1970 – Quarter-finalists

Rumania

Although the association was founded in 1910, many of the
early players in Rumanian football were in fact Hungarian.
But given the support of King Carol, a Rumanian team was
among a very small handful of European teams to compete in
the first edition of the World Cup.

In recent seasons the league has been dominated by one or
two sides, including Dynamo Bucharest, which is sponsored by
the Ministry of the Interior; Steaua, which is the team of the
Rumanian Army; and UT Arad, which has close links with
an enormous textile concern. The style of Rumanian football
has often been harsh and uncompromising, but in the past
eight or ten years, the country has produced some players of
genuine world class such as Dumitrache, Dobrin and
Dembrovski.

Wold Cup achievement:

1930 – Second in qualifying group
1934 – Beaten in first round
1938 – Beaten after play-off in first round
1950 – Did not enter
1954 – Failed to qualify
1958 – Failed to qualify
1962 – Failed to qualify
1966 – Failed to qualify
1970 – Third in group

Police on the pitch during the Italy–Chile game from the 1962 competition. Salvadore the Italian defender is in the centre, on the extreme right is Mora.

Above: World Cup 1962. Formidable winger against formidable fullback.
Garrincha (Brazil) and Wilson (England) in a duel from the quarter-final
tie which the Brazilians won 3-1.

Right: World Cup Final 1962. Djalma Santos (Brazil), Masopust
(Czechoslovakia), Didi (Brazil) and Jelinek (Czechoslovakia) in an
incident from the match that Brazil won 3-1. And where's the ball ?

BIPPA

Left: World Cup Final 1962. Mauro is unable to prevent Masopust from shooting home Czechoslovakia's only goal of the match past Gilmar, the Brazilian goalkeeper. Djalma Santos is the defender in the background.

Above: World Cup 1966. Lev Yachin making a typically acrobatic save in the Russia–West Germany semi-final. Look at this and you can understand why many people consider him the best of all post-war goalkeepers.

BIPPA

Above: World Cup 1966. The extraordinary Eusebio, in tears after Portugal's defeat by England in a thrilling semi-final tie. He would have the compensation of being the tournament's highest scorer.

Right: World Cup Final 1966. Geoff Hurst scores England's final—and his third—goal in the 4-2 victory over West Germany. Wolfang Overath is the German player nearby.

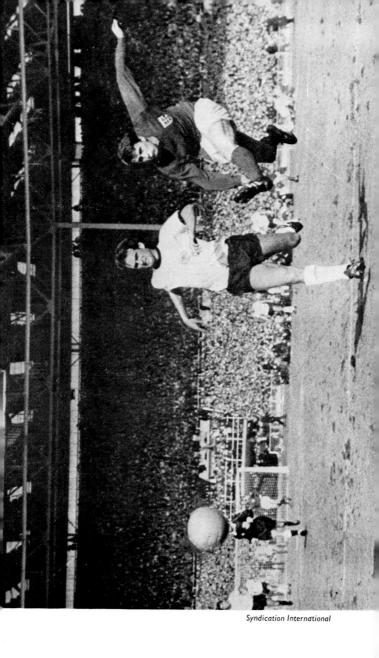

Syndication International

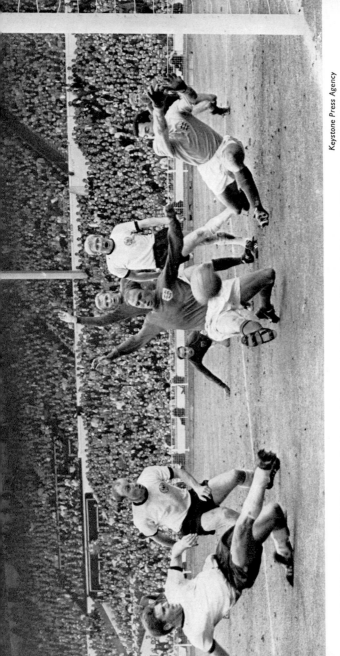

World Cup Final, 1966. With seconds of normal time remaining, Weber slides the ball home for West Germany's equalising goal. Other players shown—left to right—are : Seeler, Cohen, Wilson, Moore, Schnellinger, Banks, Jack Charlton.

World Cup 1970. Geoff Hurst's header just skimmed the post for what might have been the conclusive goal in the England—

Keystone Press Agency

Above: World Cup 1970. Uwe Seeler (left) and Franz Beckenbauer after the latter had scored the first West German goal in England's 3-2 quarter-final defeat. Seeler also played in the Tournaments of 1958, 1962 and 1966. For Beckenbauer, one of the world's most majestic players, the 1974 tournament will be his third.

Right: World Cup 1970. Gerd Muller, who would be the tournament's highest scorer, here slashes the ball past Bonetti for his side's victorious goal in the quarter-final tie against England. Prowling nearby is the English captain, Bobby Moore.

Above: World Cup 1970. Karl-Heinz Schnellinger, West Germany's famous defender playing in his fourth competition, scores the last minute equalizing goal for his country against Italy. Albertosi is the goalkeeper, Facchetti the other defender—of an Italian side that won a thrilling semi-final 4-3 after extra time.

Right: World Cup 1970. Gianni Rivera (not in picture) scores the decisive goal in the Italy—West Germany semi-final. In picture, from left : Riva, Maier, Vogts, Schnellinger, Schulz (on ground), Boninsegna.

United Press International

Syndication International

Above: World Cup 1970. Brazil's central spearhead in their victorious team–Tostao, Pelé, Jairzinho.

Right: World Cup 1970. A scene from the final, won by Brazil over Italy 4-1. Jairzinho (Brazil) by-passing the attentions of Facchetti (Italy) while Burgnich (Italy), Pelé (Brazil) and De Sisti (Italy) look on. In the background is Mazzola.

World Cup 1970. Jairzinho (centre) moments after he had scored Brazil's third goal in the final against Italy. Facchetti is the tall defender, Albertosi the beaten goalkeeper.

Russia

Football in Russia began as long ago as 1887, when two
English brothers introduced the game at their textile mill in
Crekhoro. Then came the spread of the game during the 1890's,
with the formation of a Moscow league. By 1912 Russia were
ready to enter the Olympiad.

Then came the 1917 Revolution, and a long footballing
hiatus in international terms. It was not until 1952 that the full
international team was seen again when they entered for the
1952 Olympiad; and although 1954 saw them ignoring the
World Cup, they did win the 1956 Olympic trophy. Two
years later they were in the finals of the World Cup and have
stayed there since.

Russian teams have tended to be highly drilled, often chosen
from only one or two clubs, strong in physical terms and with
a fair technical and tactical appreciation – but little flair. The
one competition in which the Russians have consistently done
well is the European Nations cup – winners in 1960; finalists
in 1964 and 1972; semi-finalists in 1968 (when they were
eliminated on the toss of a coin). Among famous Russian
players have been Lev Yachin, a goalkeeper of authority and
capable of acrobatic brilliance; and Igor Netto, an attacking
wing-half of high intelligence.

World Cup achievement:

1958 – Quarter-finalists
1962 – Quarter-finalists
1966 – Semi-finalists
1970 – Quarter-finalists

T–D

Scotland

After England the oldest association in the world, founded in
1873, even though the Queen's Park Club was formed in 1867.
It was in Scotland that the art of teamwork first came to be
perfected – for south of the border, players were too prone
to run with the ball themselves. Thus was born the Scottish
'school' of football, with its accent on quick-passing movements;
and the tradition has come down over the decades, throwing up
a myriad of fine players from that country, especially in the
'constructive' positions.

Given the talent of its players, Scotland has suffered cruelly at
two points – through bad administration, and through the fact
that so many English clubs have hived away young players on
the threshold of brilliant careers. This last factor has made it
increasingly difficult for international teams to play at full
strength and to benefit from squad training.

If the 1950's and early Sixties were dominated by Rangers,
then over the past eight years it is the Catholic Club, Celtic,
that has had its way each season; in the same period winning
one edition of the European Cup and reaching the final of
another – all under a most wise and able manager in Jock Stein.

World Cup achievement:

1950 – Refused to compete
1954 – Last in qualifying group
1958 – Last in qualifying group
1962 – Failed to qualify
1966 – Failed to qualify
1970 – Failed to qualify

Sweden

Sweden was one of the first of the Continental countries to
take up soccer as a game. As early as 1908, the Swedes
entered a team for the Olympic Games. It was heavily beaten,
but the years between the two world wars bore full testimony
to the way in which the game had caught hold in that
country. Swedish teams competed in the 1934 and 1938
World Cup finals, but it was really after the war – and under
the talented coaching of a small Yorkshireman called George
Raynor that Sweden became something of a power in world
footballing terms.

In 1950 Sweden reached the final pool of the tournament –
and strangely, when looked at in terms of strength on paper.
Two years earlier Sweden had won the Olympic football
tournament with a team that included the three Nordahl
brothers; Gunnar Gren – an inside forward of great intelligence;
and Nils Liedholm – another inside forward, who like many
of his team mates from that Olympiad would be snatched
away by wealthy Italian clubs. So, in 1950, Raynor was forced
to build again from scratch. And after 1950 he was forced
to sit quietly back while Italian clubs pillaged his best
players yet again.

Eight years later – and with many of the best players
recalled from Italian clubs for the tournament – Sweden
reached the Final, playing 'at home'. Gren was still there, as
was Leidholm; and in Kurre Hamrin, the Swedes brought
back from Italy an outside-right of verve and dazzling skills.
Another twelve years would elapse before Sweden reached
the finals again. But the talent of a small country for producing
fine players had not diminished, and Ove Kindvall remained a
central striker fit to set alongside the best in the world.

World Cup achievement:

1930 – Did not enter
1934 – Beaten in second (quarter-final) round
1938 – Semi-finalists, fourth
1950 – Final pool, third
1954 – Failed to qualify
1958 – Finalists, second
1962 – Failed to qualify
1966 – Failed to qualify
1970 – Third in qualifying pool

Uruguay

Football was introduced to Uruguay during the last years of
the last century and was monetarily encouraged by Sir Thomas
Lipton, the tea millionaire who donated the Lipton Cup for
annual games between Uruguay and the Argentine.

For a country with a present population of only four
million, the achievement in international terms has been
remarkable. Twice winners of the Olympic title – in 1924
(when they beat Switzerland 3-0) and 1928 (when they beat
Argentina in a replayed Final 2-1) – and twice winners of the
World Cup, Uruguay have given so much to the game. Not
surprisingly the league is dominated by the two metropolitan
clubs of Montevideo – Penarol and Nacional. And if in recent
years the game there has hardened, then that hardness has been
added to consummate skills in ball-play and fine tactical
intelligence.

World Cup achievement:

1930 – Winners
1934 – Refused to enter
1938 – Refused to enter
1950 – Winners
1954 – Semi-finalists, fourth
1958 – Failed to qualify
1962 – Third in qualifying group
1966 – Quarter-finalists
1970 – Semi-finalists, fourth.

West Germany

Football there began at the end of the last century, in the universities, and much encouraged by local entrepreneurs. The association was founded in 1900, the game grew quickly, and by the time the World Cup competition began, the Germans were very much an international force to be reckoned with.

It has been since the war, however, that the game has been most impressive. Under the wily manager Sepp Herberger, the German team won the 1954 World Cup, always provided difficult opposition; and under Helmut Schoen (who had served as assistant to Herberger for some time), came further triumphs. The performances of the German national team over the past year or two have left no one in doubt that it will start out as favourite for the Munich edition of the World Cup, studded with stars of great talent and able to practise a type of free and collective football that only comes from truly great teams. Well-drilled and cunning, German teams have always striven for intuitive brilliance – and now they appear to have the type of players who can provide the golden finish.

World Cup achievement:

1934 – Semi-finalists, third
1938 – Beaten in first round
1950 – Barred from entry
1954 – Winners
1958 – Semi-finalists, fourth
1962 – Quarter-finalists
1966 – Finalists, second
1970 – Semi-finalists, third.

There, then are some of the teams who may shine this summer.
More important, I wonder what this edition of the World Cup
will throw up in tactical terms. In 1958 it was the Brazilians
who introduced the world to 4-2-4; in 1962 they went out
and played 4-3-3, with Zagalo pulled firmly back into midfield.
That was the system used by England in 1966 – though it
could be claimed that both Alan Ball and Martin Peters were
given rôles that were more flexible than that of midfield
providers. In 1970 the Brazilians played a curious 4-3½-2½
with Rivelino left to rove down the left of the field as midfield
provider and as finisher.

What we are likely to see in Munich from one or two teams
at least is 10-0-0, or 0-10-0 or 0-0-10 – that is to say, play
that is fluid, a system by which defenders attack and attackers
defend. Some years ago Sir Alf Ramsey described Martin
Peters as being a player 'ten years ahead of his time'. It was a
quote that came childishly to be used against him whenever
Peters had a bad game, but the point stands, and Peters remains
a player of infinite resource and resilience.

Whatever the system, we can hope for the best in the belief
that there are enough teams there to provide for it, to overcome
the negative tactics that certain teams are likely to use. There
are many examples of fine teams who have lost World Cup
matches and bequeathed to the game more than their victors.
It's a lesson worth remembering.

4 SOME OF THE WORLD'S LEADING PLAYERS

Where on earth do you start? How on earth can you suggest everything that ought to be suggested. No section such as this would ever have included Nobby Stiles; and yet a man of his extraordinary qualities should have been given pride of place. 'Style' so often has to be the main criterion.

Let's just say that here are short portraits of some of those players who will, hopefully, be displaying their skills in West Germany during the summer. Some play for countries which are 'seeded' to reach the final pool; others for countries with little chance of shining. Perhaps one ought also to spare space for those who have never played in the final stages of a World Cup tournament. Think of George Best, of Denis Law, of Jim Baxter; think of Pat Jennings, who over the past few seasons has firmly established himself as one of the best three or four goalkeepers in the world, and who may never get the chance to display his skills against the broader canvas of a Final tournament. One hopes he will; but that is a hope against history.

If there are fewer British players mentioned here than many would like to see, then I suggest that that is as it should be. Compared to that in most countries, our footballing press is parochial in the extreme. Go to Italy, to Germany, to Brazil, to Scandinavia and the knowledge of the man in the street or the fan in the local bar is altogether more catholic than that of his British counterpart. These are countries where there are daily sports papers of prestige, papers whose coverage of sport in all its forms is truly 'world-wide'. Ask the Italian football fan for information as to the final placings in last season's English First Division and he may well have it at the front of his mind. Stop a fan on the way to Old Trafford or Stamford

Bridge, Elland Road or The Dell and ask him how it was that
Juventus won the Italian league title for the second year in
succession, and he'll gaze at you blankly, call you a 'daft
monkey' or kick you up the backside – depending which side
he got out of bed that morning and which team his heroes are
facing that particular afternoon. (For those who are interested:
A.C. Milan went into the final day of that championship needing
a good result against a lowly and talentless team – and lost.)

There is that argument – and there is the argument of truth.
Most footballing magazines, most daily newspapers feed us all
with a mass of material about British players – enough,
certainly, to assuage the appetites of those who love nothing
more than facts and figures. But all things are comparative, and
there is nothing so healthy as the occasional shock that brings
people back to earth. And so we get back to where we started –
a plea to realize that not all our geese are swans, that
throughout the world there is a plenitude of fine players whose
reputations often stand or fall in our eyes by what they
achieve in World Cup competitions, that when all the yapping
is done there is only a small clutch of British players who
deserve a pride of place in the gallery of great players who have
graced the game.

So – this is a brief (certainly too brief) look at some of the
most talented players of the recent past and the present. If only
half of them play next summer with all the skill at their
command, we may be in for a feast of good football. If.

And just a gentle reminder. In Brazil there are many people
who can claim to have seen a fair proportion of the best
individual performances thrown up by Leonidas before the
war and Pelé after. Not too long ago an enterprising character
carried out a straw poll of such people with the question
'Who was the greatest player you ever saw?' It was Leonidas
who received sixty per cent of the vote, Pelé forty per cent.

Food for thought, there; and a neat example of how powerful
are the suggestions put out by the mass media. One is left
wishing that television had been commonplace in the time of
Leonidas, of Monti, Sarosi, Stabile, Meazza, Piola and company
before the war; of Julinho, Schiaffino, Puskas, Liedholm and
company after the war.

Pietro ANASTASI (Italy). Born 7th April 1948, a Sicilian who
first made his name with Varese before being transferred to
Juventus for a world record fee of well over £400,000 in the
summer of 1968. Beautifully balanced, with a penchant for the
spectacular close to goal, he was originally chosen in the
Italian party for the 1970 World Cup finals but had to
withdraw through illness. Has recently played in a more
deep-lying rôle for his club, and his international appearances
have been too limited.

Franz BECKENBAUER (West Germany). Born 11th September
1945 and undoubtedly one of the most elegant players ever
to tread an international pitch. He was on the books of
Bayern Munich at the age of thirteen, went on to win schoolboy
and youth caps. Debut for the full international side came in
September 1965, since when he has become recognized as a
player of the highest class, both in midfield and as an attacking
'sweeper' – which is his preferred position. Played in the 1966
and 1970 Finals, led West Germany to triumph in the 1972
European Nations Cup tournament. Often wasted in a tight-
marking rôle (particularly in the 1966 Final), he has now
asserted himself as a player whose technical brilliance needs
to be given the fullest rein. Voted European Footballer of the
Year in 1972.

Oleg BLOKHINE (Russia). Aged 21. His mother was a national
sprint champion and this fair-haired left-winger began his
sporting life in her foosteps. Although he still likes to train
with, and run against Valeri Borzov (Olympic champion at
both sprint distances), Blokhine has become the best Russian
footballer of his generation with phenomenal acceleration,
brilliant ball-control and a fulminating shot. Studies biology
at the University of Kiev, his native town. Height: 5ft 10ins;
weight 11st.

Paul BREITNER (West Germany). Born 5th September 1951,
and joined Bayern Munich in the summer of 1970. His first
cap followed a year later. A leading member of West
Germany's team in their successful 1972 season, Breitner is a
defensive player with all the qualities of a powerful midfield
prompter – clever sense of positioning, plenty of fire, good in
the tackle, fine sense of timing. Admires the works of Marx
and Lenin.

Billy BREMNER (Scotland). Aged 29. Fiery midfield performer
with Leeds United, whom he has captained to many triumphs
in recent seasons. First international cap came in 1965; since
then Bremner has established himself as a player whom
Scotland cannot do without. His enormous vitality, his drive,
his pride make him a fierce competitor. Too few acknowledge
that he is also one of the most gifted players in the game
today, with the ability to deliver defence-splitting passes and
when the occasion arises to score good goals. Munich should
provide him with his first taste of finals competition in a
World Cup tournament. Height 5ft 6ins; weight 10st 2lbs.

Paulo CESAR (Brazil). Aged 23. Flamboyant, debonair midfield
player who did well as a reserve in Mexico and since Pelé's

'retirement' has become a key figure in the national team. A
player of high speed, deadly shot in either foot, superb
dribbling ability and a fine talent for bending freekicks.
Extremely effective on wings as well as in centre.

Johann CRUYFF (Holland). Aged 27. Voted European
Footballer of the year in 1971, a player of extraordinary
reflex and skill. Made his debut for Ajax Amsterdam in the
1965-66 season, went on with them to lose one European
Cup Final, win three others. Suspended for a year by the Dutch
Federation for 'ungentlemanly conduct' early in his career, he
has now harnessed his natural talent to determination.
Widely thought-of as the world's most gifted player, and
symbol of the modern, affluent breed of player with a fair
number of business interests outside the game.

Florea DUMITRACHE (Rumania). Aged 25. Came on to the
international scene just before the Mexico tournament, where
he disappointed. But he is a player of great mobility, roving
the pitch in search of space within which to express his
great talents on the ball. Can score spectacular goals.

Dragan DZAJIC (Yugoslavia). Aged 28. An outside-left with
brilliant ball control and deadly finishing power. Made a
decisive contribution when his national team reached the final
of the European Nations Cup tournament of 1968. Selected to
play for the Rest of the World against Brazil the following
November. Broke left leg in March 1973.

GERSON de Oliveira Nunes (Brazil). Born 11th January 1941,
he played for Brazil in the Olympiad of 1960. Just prior to the
1962 World Cup finals he broke a leg; but played in the 1966
tournament; and brilliantly, in that of Mexico four years later.

A chain-smoker, Gerson is often accused of being unable to
last the full ninety minutes of a game, accused also of bearing
too dilettante an approach towards important matches. Lethal
with a dead ball, he scored a spectacular goal for his country
in the 1970 Final against Italy in open play. Height 5ft 8ins;
weight 11st 5lbs.

JAIRZINHO (Brazil). Aged 29. Real name: Jair Ventura Filho.
Made his international debut in 1964; played for Brazil in the
1966 World Cup; and, decisively, in 1970 where he
established a record by scoring in each of Brazil's six games.
In the Brazilian Independence tournament of 1972 he was
again on punishing form. Nominally a right-winger, he
prefers – and is more effective in – the rôle of central striker.
One of the world's greatest forwards. Height: 5ft 8ins;
weight 11st 5lbs.

Murtaz KHURTSILAVA (Russia). Aged 30. Central defender,
who for years has partnered the great Albert Shesternev, though
has a reputation more for close marking than commanding
the back line of the defence. Made his international debut in
the 1966 World Cup tournament; also played in Mexico four
years later. Soviet footballer of the year in 1968, but has been
troubled by injuries in recent seasons. Height 5ft 10ins;
weight 12st 2lbs.

Ove KINDVALL (Sweden). Aged 30. Like so many Swedish stars
Kindvall has been forced to play much of his football away
from his country, most notably for Feyenoord, the
European Cup winners in 1970. A small, athletic centre-forward
who runs intelligently off the ball, he possesses good
shooting power, the ability to dovetail well with colleagues,
great acceleration. Height 5ft. 7ins; weight 10st. 13lbs.

Roger MAGNUSSON (Sweden). Born 20th March 1945. One
of the most fascinating of European players. He is a
ball-playing winger of fine ability, whose career has been
chequered from the first. As a teenager he played a short
season with the Brazilian club, Flamengo. Soon afterwards
he found himself being transferred to Juventus, the wealthy
Italian club; who transferred him to the German team,
Cologne, when the Italian league refused to widen the rules
regarding foreign players. Juventus recalled him the following
season (1967–68) as a reserve de luxe, using him only in
European Cup games. Following this Magnusson found his
way into French football, where he remains. He stands as a
playing testament to the many difficulties that beset the game
in Sweden – the long winters, the lack of money. But a fine
player, nevertheless, a worthy successor to Hamrin on Sweden's
right wing, possessor of a dizzying swerve.

Oscar MAS (Argentina). Aged 28. Chunky winger who played
excellently during Argentina's ill-fated search for fame in
1966. He has for years been one of the most renowned of
South American footballers – his ball-control delicate, his
ability to penetrate harsh defences acute. The Argentinians had
a sweep-out following their failure to qualify in 1970, but Mas
remained one of the 'veteran' players whose services seemed
indispensable.

Ladislao MAZURKIEWICZ (Uruguay). Born 14th December
1945. As his name would suggest, of Polish ancestry. It may
be that this very fine goalkeeper will not be chosen for the
Munich finals. Certainly he was mysteriously and mistakenly
omitted from the Uruguayan squad for the 1972 Brazilian
Independence tournament. For a long time he was a leader of
the Uruguayan players' union, an eager militant on behalf of

players' rights. Absolutely excellent in the tournaments of
1966 (in which he played at the age of 20 – abnormally young
for an international goalkeeper) and 1970. Height 5ft 9ins;
weight 12st 6lbs.

Sandro MAZZOLA (Italy). Born 8th November 1942. Son of
the famous Italian international, Valentino, who perished
along with his Torino team mates in the Superga air disaster
of 1949. Well on the way to setting a record for the number
of international appearances in an Italian jersey, Mazzola is a
midfield player of great stamina and virtuosity. Played in the
1966 tournament; and excellent in that of 1970 where his
hard running and imaginative prompting was one of the few
Italian highlights in the Final against Brazil. A leading member
of the victorious Internazionale (Milan) side of the mid-
Sixties. Height 5ft 9ins; weight 10st 12lbs.

Bobby MOORE (England). Aged 32. By general concensus the
best defender on view in the tournaments of 1966 (when he
captained England to victory) and 1970. A player of great
footballing intelligence and authority, his performances for
England over a decade have been wonderfully consistent in
their brilliance. Made his England debut just prior to the 1962
tournament, in which he played with distinction; captained
England for the first of many games against East Germany in
1963. Voted Player of the tournament in 1966. Holder of F.A.
Cup Winners medal (1964) and European Cup Winners Cup
medal (1965) – both with West Ham, his only club. No one
'reads' a game more astutely than he, and his performances in
Mexico were simply brilliant. A truly remarkable footballer,
who has won vast respect throughout the world for his sporting
attitude and sporting skills. Height 6ft; weight 12st 12lbs.

Gerd MULLER (West Germany), Born 3rd November 1945.
Signed for Bayern Munich in 1964. European Footballer of the
Year in 1970, following his fine success in the Mexico
tournament where he came out as leading scorer with ten
goals. A deadly finisher, with excellent technique and the
ability to dart quickly into precise positions. Four times in
international matches he has scored four goals; and indeed his
goal-scoring statistics are paralysingly high. Tough and
resilient, his goals have helped Bayern win the German Cup,
the championship and the European Cup Winners' Cup – this
last in 1967. Height 5ft 9ins; weight 12st 4lbs.

Gunter NETZER (West Germany). Born 14th September 1944
in München Gladbach. Has played most of his football for local
clubs. Signed by Borussia at the start of the 1963-64 season;
in the German forty for the 1966 tournament but did not
travel to England; in the German twenty-two for Mexico, but
did not play a game. A vital member, however, of West
Germany's successful 1972 team. His brilliant ball control,
piercing eye for an opening, genius with freekicks make him
a formidable player. Another player – like Cruyff – cast in the
modern mould. Serious and intelligent. Transferred to
Real Madrid in the summer of 1973.

Edson Arantes Nascimento PELÉ (Brazil). Aged 33. He has
officially retired from international football, but one wonders
whether his extraordinary powers won't be needed by the
Brazilians in Munich. It is not merely what this exceptional
player can perform in his own right that matters, but also the
uplifting effect his presence has to other members of his team.
Made his international debut at the age of sixteen, in 1957;
came to Sweden as a member of the victorious Brazilian side
in the 1958 tournament where the world at large witnessed his

amazing gymnastic skills. A muscle injury curtailed operations
in the tournament of 1962; and four years later he was
cynically fouled out of Brazil's game against Portugal. But in
1970 he was back, his genius evident to everyone. Scored his
one thousandth goal in senior football in 1969. Height 5ft
8½ins; weight 12st.

Luigi RIVA (Italy). Born 7th November 1944. The man whom
Pelé described as the most dangerous finisher in the world
just prior to the 1970 World Cup finals. There, deprived of
adequate attention from his midfield players, Riva disappointed
the legion of people who had expected from him truly great
things. Twice (and twice in international matches) he has
broken a leg; but still he comes back, his left foot the most
fearsome to be seen since the retirement of Puskas. Deadly
with freekicks, a genuine opportunist who wears the number
eleven shirt but is fundamentally a central attacker. First cap,
June 1965. Up there with Meazza and Piola as a chief goalscorer
in international competition for Italy. Retiring and modest,
three times chief goal-scorer in the Italian league for his club,
Cagliari, in Sardinia. Cagliari were reputed to have turned
down an offer for Riva's services that amounted to little less
than a million pounds sterling. Height 5ft 10; weight 11st
7lbs.

Roberto RIVELINO (Brazil). Aged 28. Came on to the
international scene in 1968 when he toured Europe with the
Brazilian team and played for Brazil against the Rest of the
World that November, scoring the first of the Brazilian goals.
Deadly with freekicks, played well in patches during the
Mexico finals; a fine tactician and thinker whose main
weakness seems to be an inability to last the pace of a hard
game. Height 5ft 8ins; weight 11st 1lb.

Gianni RIVERA (Italy). Born 18th August 1943. Played in
tournaments of 1962 (aged eighteen), 1966 and 1970. A
midfield general of great technical accomplishment, the ability
to strike a ball vast distances with imagination and pinpoint
accuracy, Rivera can also score goals – as evinced by the fact
that he came out equal first among Italian scorers during the
1972-73 League season. First cap in May 1962, after having
made his league debut at the age of fifteen. The true 'Golden
Boy' of Italian football over a decade, Rivera has too often
been pilloried by the international selectors, his style of play
making him a perfect scapegoat whenever anything goes
wrong. It is not in his nature to play the bustling midfield
provider, rather to probe for weaknesses in opposing defences
with those razor-like passes of his. Did well in Mexico, despite
being forced to play as a counter to Mazzola – whose style is
different, but probably complementary. Winner of league
championship, Italian Cup, European Cup and Cup Winners
Cup medals, he also led his club, A.C. Milan, to victory over
Estudiantes of South America in the 1969 edition of the
'Trans-continental' cup. European Footballer of the Year in
1969. Likes to speak his mind – a trait that has often led him
to trouble with Italian administrators. Height 5ft 9ins; weight
10st 12lbs.

Pedro ROCHA (Uruguay). Aged 30. Won first cap in 1962;
represented Uruguay in World Cup finals of 1962, 1966 and
1970 – where he was injured after only a dozen minutes of
the first game in which he played and took no further part in
the tournament. Tall, elegant midfield player with fine control
and incisive eye for an opening, he can also score goals that
are spectacular. Height 5ft 11ins; weight 12st 6lbs.

Peter SHILTON (England). Aged 23. Considered good enough
by his club, Leicester City, at the age of sixteen to allow them
to sell Gordon Banks. Shilton takes after Banks in many respects
– in the sureness of his handling, in his taciturn manner, in
physical characteristics. Understudied Banks in the national
team for two or three years, took over when the former
international was injured in a car crash. Safe, and when the
calling arises, very agile. Height 6ft; weight 12st 10lbs.

Eduardo Goncales Andrade TOSTAO (Brazil). Aged 27. Student
of economics. Made his international debut just prior to the
1966 finals, in which he played with fair success. Just prior
to the 1970 finals was operated on in America for detached
retina. Recovered sight and confidence to emerge as a genuine
super-star, a player of delicate ball control, fine intelligence
and with a good shot. Eye trouble has recurred and it may be
that the Brazilians will renounce the man who has come to be
known as 'The White Pelé' – which will be sad. One hopes
that he will play in Munich and that the world can marvel
again at his uncanny anticipation. Height 5ft 8½ins; weight
11st 5lbs.

Berti Hans-Hubert VOGTS (West Germany). Born 30 December
1946. A fullback of great authority who played decisively well
in Mexico in 1970. Has recently been pushed forward into
more of a midfield rôle with his club, Borussia
München Gladbach. But in either position his excellent
tackling and canny distribution makes him one of the world's
best defensive players. Height 5ft 7ins; weight 10st 12lbs.

Dino ZOFF (Italy). Born 28th February 1942. Tall, courteous
goalkeeper of great skill who played for Udinese, Mantova and

Napoli before being transferred to Juventus of Turin in the
summer of 1972. In the Italian side that won the European
Nations Cup in 1968; a reserve in the Mexico finals of 1970,
but soon regained his place. Set record by playing 903
minutes of Italian league football without conceding a goal.
Played for Common Market against Britain (with Denmark and
Eire) in January 1973. Height 6ft; weight 12st 12lbs.

5   SOME STATISTICS

Number of Entries

1930 – 13
1934 – 29
1938 – 25
1950 – 29
1954 – 35
1958 – 51 (four countries withdrew without playing a game)
1962 – 56 (three countries withdrew without playing a game)
1966 – 53
1970 – 71
1974 – 81 (four countries withdrew without playing a game)

Attendances at Final matches

URUGUAY 1930 – 90,000 (Montevideo)
ITALY 1934 – 50,000 (Rome)
FRANCE 1938 – 45,000 (Paris)
BRAZIL 1950 – 200,000 (record) (Rio de Janeiro)
SWITZERLAND 1954 – 60,000 (Berne)
SWEDEN 1958 – 50,000 (Stockholm)
CHILE 1962 – 70,000 (Santiago)
ENGLAND 1966 – 100,000 (Wembley Stadium, London)
MEXICO 1970 – 112,000 (Mexico City)

Use of players

Brazil hold the record for the least number of players used in
a World Cup winning team throughout a final series. In 1962
they needed only twelve players to defend their title
successfully: Gilmar, Santos (D.), Santos (N.), Mauro, Zizimo,
Zito, Didì, Vavà, Garrincha, Zagalo – who played in all six
games; Pelé, who played in two; and Amarildo, who played
in four.

Other winners, with the number of players used as follows:

1930 Uruguay – 16
1934 Italy – 17
1938 Italy – 14
1950 Uruguay – 14
1954 West Germany – 19
1958 Brazil – 16
1966 England – 15 (Connelly, Greaves, Paine, Callaghan in
                    addition to the winning team)
1970 Brazil – 14

Leading Scorers

1930   STABILE (Argentina) 8
        CEA (Uruguay) 5

1934   SCHIAVIO (Italy) 4
        NEJEDLY (Czechoslovakia) 4
        CONEN (Germany) 4

1938   LEONIDAS (Brazil) 8
        SZENGELLER (Hungary) 7
        PIOLA (Italy) 5

1950 ADEMIR (Brazil) 7
      SCHIAFFINO (Uruguay) 5
      BASORA (Spain) 5

1954 KOCSIS (Hungary) 11
      PROBST (Austria) 6
      MORLOCK (West Germany) 6

1958 FONTAINE (France) 13
      PELÉ (Brazil) 6
      RAHN (West Germany) 6
      VAVÀ (Brazil) 5

1962 ALBERT (Hungary) 4
      GARRINCHA (Brazil) 4
      VAVÀ (Brazil) 4
      SANCHEZ (Chile) 4
      JERKOVIC (Yugoslavia) 4
      IVANOV (Russia) 4

1966 EUSEBIO (Portugal) 9
      HALLER (West Germany) 5
      HURST (England) 4
      BECKENBAUER (West Germany) 4
      PORKUIAN (Russia) 4

1970 MULLER (West Germany) 10
      JAIRZINHO (Brazil) 7*
      CUBILLAS (Peru) 5
      PELÉ (Brazil) 4
      BISHOVETS (Russia) 4

*Jairzinho scored in each of the six rounds

Other goal-scoring statistics: Hurst (England) remains the only man
so far to score a hat trick of goals in a Final.

The highest individual scoring feat in a World Cup Final
tournament match is four. Eight players have achieved this:
Wetterstroem (Sweden) v Cuba 1938; Leonidas (Brazil)
v Poland 1938; Willimowski (Poland) v Brazil 1938; Ademir
(Brazil) v Sweden 1950; Schiaffino (Uruguay) v Bolivia (1950);
Kocsis (Hungary) v West Germany 1954; Fontaine (France)
v West Germany 1958; and Eusebio (Portugal) v North
Korea 1966.

*Pooled together the best individual totals in World Cup tournaments go
like this:*

13 Fontaine (France) 1958
11 Kocsis (Hungary) 1954
10 Muller (West Germany) 1970
 9 Eusebio (Portugal) 1966
 8 Stabile (Argentine) 1930;
      Leonidas (Brazil) 1938
 7 Szengeller (Hungary) 1938;
      Ademir (Brazil) 1950
      Jairzinho (Brazil) 1970;
 6 Probst (Austria) 1954;
      Morlock (West Germany) 1954;
      Pelé (Brazil) 1958;
      Rahn (West Germany) 1958.

Total Number of Goals Scored in World Cup Final Stages

1930   70 goals in 18 matches
1934   70 goals in 17 matches
1938   81 goals in 18 matches
1950   90 goals in 22 matches
1954   135 goals in 26 matches
1958   119 goals in 35 matches
1962   89 goals in 32 matches
1966   89 goals in 32 matches
1970   95 goals in 32 matches

The Trophy

The Jules Rimet Trophy – won outright by the Brazilians in
1970 by virtue of their third victory – was designed by the
French sculptor, Abel Lafleur, stood a foot high and weighed
in the region of nine pounds of gold. The new trophy – to
be competed for for the first time in 1974 and known as the
FIFA World Cup – has been designed by an Italian sculptor,
Silvio Gazzaniga, cost £8,000, is made of eighteen-carat gold
and weighs in the region of ten pounds. All participating
countries will receive a small replica of this trophy.

Changes in format

For the first time in the history of the competition since 1950, the knockout element will be eliminated next summer. Teams will compete in groups – four teams to each of the four groups; and the two top teams in each group will go forward to the second round of group matches. Only the Final itself will be on a knockout basis, that played between the leading teams in each of the secondary groups.

Tickets

2,129,000 have been issued for the thirty-eight matches due to take place next summer.